# Never and Always

*Micronesian Legends, Fables and Folklore*

*by*
*The Students of*
*The Community College*
*of Micronesia*

*Compiled and Edited*
*by Gene Ashby*

*Illustrated*
*by Thomas Joel*

**RAINY DAY PRESS**
**Pohnpei, F.S.M.**     **Eugene, Oregon**

*There are more things in heaven
and earth, Horatio,
Than are dreamt in your philosophy.*
            Hamlet
            Act. 1, Scene 5

First Condensed Edition Published by
Rainy Day Press, 1983

Second Expanded Edition
Published in 1989

Copyright © by Rainy Day Press
All Rights Reserved

Library of Congress Catalog Card Number:
89-51110

International Standard Book Number:
0-931742-11-0

Published by Rainy Day Press

P.O. Box 574
Kolonia, Pohnpei, F.S.M. 96941

1147 East 26th Ave.
Eugene, Oregon 97403

Printed in U.S.A.

*Gina Marie...*
   *for you.*

# *Acknowledgements*

The students and former students of the Community College of Micronesia on Pohnpei made this anthology possible, and certainly deserve the most credit. Ms. Iris Falcam, Librarian at C.C.M., again rescued the editor from myriad mistakes by providing her time to proofread the manuscript and by offering suggestions.

The title *Never and Always* is borrowed from a line in a poem by Gottfried Benn, "Palau," (circa 1925). Of the eighty-six stories included in the book, ten have been used in two other Rainy Day Press publications, *Pohnpei, An Island Argosy* or *Micronesian Customs and Beliefs*. They are included again here because they are too good to leave out of an anthology of legends about Micronesia.

The illustrations of Micronesian objects and scenes were drawn by Thomas Joel, a former student at C.C.M. Originally from Mwoakilloa, Joel was educated in Yap before attending college on Pohnpei.

The layout for the book was done under the supervision of Dennis Hunt, Editing & Design Services, Eugene, Oregon. Mike Helm, publisher of Rainy Day Press, again assisted with suggestions and advice.

And finally, many thanks to the imaginations of islanders, past and present, young and old. And very special appreciation is extended to all ghosts (both male and female), demigods, demons and monsters, giants and giant clams, sea-lizards, magicians, and local rogues, rascals and heroes, for being the characters around which Micronesian myths, legends, fables and folklore have been created.

# *Student Writers*

Anthony Albert
Swithson Alik
Gina Always
Koncy Ampros
Ignathio Berag
Miter Bernard
Kaspar Berry
Faunny Blunt
Mercy Choram
Jonas Dauny
Sinceria Eas
Thomas Edyn
Juanita Fagel
Joe Felix
Ketsen Fritz
Teresa Gamabruw
Salome George
Jorlang Gideon
Joe Habuchmai
Roy Hainrick
Eddy Haleyalig
Johnny Hedson
Raymond Henry
Raymond Igechep
Robert Jackson
Elias Johnny
Macnald Jonah
Robert Jonas
Maria Jose
Evelyn Joseph

Irwin Kiahd
Esetong Kimiuo
Miske Kony
Melvin Jaej
Ignathio Letolgam
Susan Ligow
Stephen Marcus
Keep Maruame
Exley Meyar
Hiram Malolo
Emius Nena
Robert Petalmai
Rencelly Phillip
Memorina Ponum
Willy Radolfetheg
Winifred Recheungel
Ramon Retwaiut
Benedict Rikin
Josua Ruben
Robert Ruwan
Thomas Santos
Margarita Scaliem
Tobias Shirano
Ignacia Soram
Livingston Taulung
Helmer Tawos
Peter Tharngan
Theodosia Ulenghong
Thomas Wichilbuch

# Contents

Acknowledgements .................................................... vi
Student Writers ...................................................... vii
Preface .............................................................. xiii
Mokil or Mwoakilloa? ................................................. xvi

## I. *The Origins of Islands and Peoples*
### Palau Islands
How the Islands Were Separated ................................. 3
### Yap Islands
The Day that Waab Became Yap ................................... 4
Why Sipin Disappeared Under the Sea ............................ 5
How the Yap Islands Were Separated ............................. 6
How Yap Became Populated ....................................... 8
How a Part of Yap Was Claimed by a Trick ...................... 10
### Yap Outliers
How Ulithi Was Formed .......................................... 11
The Discovery of an Undersea Island ............................ 12
Why Fasu Disappeared from Ifalik ............................... 14
How Gaferut Was Raised from the Sea ............................ 15
### Truk Islands
How a Mountain on Tol Became Islets ............................ 17
How Pisiiras Was Raised from the Sea ........................... 17

| | |
|---|---|
| Why Fano Split Away from Moen | 19 |
| How an Islet Was Pushed Away from Udot | 19 |
| Why a Part of Uman Was Moved to Murilo | 21 |
| How Unanu Became Populated | 22 |

### Truk Outliers

| | |
|---|---|
| The Ghost Woman of Nomwin | 24 |
| How Lukunor Became Populated | 26 |
| Why Piafo Was Moved to Lukunor | 27 |
| How the Islets of Ettal Were Formed | 28 |

### Pohnpei Island

| | |
|---|---|
| The Origins of Pohnpei | 29 |
| The Demigod Builders of Nan Madol | 31 |
| How Langar Was Formed | 33 |

### Pohnpei Outliers

| | |
|---|---|
| How Mwoakilloa Was Raised from the Sea | 33 |
| The Discovery and Populating of Pingelap | 35 |
| How Touhou at Kapingamarangi Was Built | 36 |

### Kosrae Island

| | |
|---|---|
| How Kosrae Villages Were First Populated and Named | 37 |

### Marshall Islands

| | |
|---|---|
| Why Kwajalein Has Separate Islets | 39 |

## II. The Origins of Reefs, Waters and Landmarks

### Palau Islands

| | |
|---|---|
| How a Pool Lost Its Spell at Ngerdmau | 43 |
| Why Stone Figures Appear at Ngermid | 44 |

### Yap Islands

| | |
|---|---|
| The First Stone Money of Yap | 45 |

### Yap Outliers

| | |
|---|---|
| The Red Coral of Eauripik | 47 |
| The Rock of Khlop on Satawan | 48 |
| Why Coconut Trees Are Prominent on Woleai | 51 |
| How Taro Was First Brought to Woleai | 52 |

### Truk Islands

| | |
|---|---|
| The Tunnel of Paata | 54 |

| | |
|---|---:|
| How an Octopus Formed a Mountain on Moen | 55 |
| **Truk Outliers** | |
| Why Sand Was Exchanged for Soil on Murilo | 56 |
| The Sweet Water of East Fayu | 56 |
| How Coconut Crabs Came to East Fayu | 59 |
| How Namoluk Lost Its Brave Warriors | 60 |
| How a Sandbar Was Formed on Losap | 61 |
| The Large Papaya of Nama | 63 |
| Why a Brother and Sister Were Turned to Stone | 64 |
| Why a Reef Was Formed at Satawan | 66 |
| Why a Channel Appears on Ettal | 67 |
| **Pohnpei Island** | |
| The Giants and the Tridacna Shells | 67 |
| How Sokehs Rock Was Formed | 68 |
| Naruhpe's Pool in Madolenihmw | 70 |
| **Pohnpei Outliers** | |
| How a River Was Stolen from Mwoakilloa | 71 |
| The Ghost-Rock of Mwoakilloa Lagoon | 72 |
| The Stingray's Crevice on Mwoakilloa | 73 |
| Why the Islets of Pingelap Are Separated | 74 |
| **Kosrae Island** | |
| The Stone Footprints at Walung | 75 |
| The Sleeping Woman and the Whale | 76 |
| Why Sharks Smell of Urine | 78 |
| Revenge on a Cruel King | 79 |
| How a Channel Was Formed on Kosrae | 81 |
| **Marshall Islands** | |
| Why Sharks Inhabit Lowakalle Reef | 83 |
| Why People Avoid Adrie at Kwajalein | 85 |
| How Reefs Were Formed on Majuro | 86 |
| How a Large Pool was Formed on Mejit | 87 |

## III. Stories of Customs, Skills and Values
### Palau Islands

| | |
|---|---:|
| Why a Girl Became a Dugong | 91 |

| | |
|---|---:|
| Why Bats and Rats Are Alike | 93 |
| Why Pregnant Women Receive Special Care | 94 |
| **Yap Islands** | |
| How Net Fishing Was Learned at Gagil | 94 |
| How Obedience Saved a Voyage | 96 |
| **Yap Outliers** | |
| How Trap Fishing Was Learned on Olimarao | 99 |
| How Falalep Was Captured by Losiep | 100 |
| **Truk Islands** | |
| Why Sharks Are Feared on Tol | 101 |
| **Truk Outliers** | |
| Why the Islet of Ames Was Destroyed | 102 |
| How Fishing Methods Were Learned on Lukunor | 104 |
| **Pohnpei Island** | |
| The First Sakau Plant on Pohnpei | 106 |
| A Bird and a Stolen Soul | 107 |
| How Deception Saved U | 108 |
| How Pohnpei Was Conquered | 109 |
| An Ungrateful Boy and a Turtle | 111 |
| **Pohnpei Outliers** | |
| The Female People-Eater of Pakin | 112 |
| Lodup of Mwoakilloa | 113 |
| The First Chief of Pingelap | 114 |
| Why Coconut Trees Flourish at Paina on Sapwuahfik | 116 |
| Why Flounder Fish Are Flat | 118 |
| **Kosrae Island** | |
| How the Giants Were Killed by Niforok | 119 |
| How Unkindness Was Repaid on Kosrae | 121 |
| Why Cats Hate Dogs | 122 |
| **Marshall Islands** | |
| How Fire Came to Likiep | 123 |
| Related Readings | 127 |

# *Preface*

An anthology is literally defined as "a gathering of flowers." The bouquet of literature written by Micronesians, however, is quite small, and most published writings from the area have been produced by outsiders. Part of the difficulty lies in the fact that children grow up speaking eight different vernacular languages in the three million square miles of the Western Pacific that geographers define as Micronesia. For nearly all of the people living in the islands, English has been a second and often a third language.

*Never and Always* with its companion volume *Micronesian Customs and Beliefs*, written by students at the Community College of Micronesia, is the largest body of published writing in English by Micronesians. Many of the original versions of the myths, legends, fables and folklore that follow can be traced to a preliterate era, which in most of Micronesia was a short century and a half ago. The following stories, however, were written in English by quite literate Micronesian college students on Pohnpei. The original purpose of the stories was for instruction or entertainment, and they were meant to be communicated orally. Orthographies were first developed to write the spoken gospel into written vernacular languages, and very un-Christian demons, demigods, ghosts and monsters were quite low on the translation-priority list of the first missionary arrivals. Most of the following stories appear in print in this anthology for the first time.

Micronesians permanently inhabit about a hundred of the 2,141 atolls, islets and islands in the Western Pacific that are spread over a watery area the size of the continental United States. Yet, one finds many more similarities than differences in the characters, plots and themes of the folktales of islanders. Culture, geography and social order on islands in Micronesia are similar despite vast distances and linguistic differences. More variety might appear in stories from the high islands because of a greater diffusion of ecology and culture than on atolls, but many of the stories from the Marshall Islands in the east would not be unfamiliar to a Palauan living three thousand miles away in the west.

The themes of Micronesian stories are universal: good versus evil; heroism, and success of the underdog; the consequences for children of disobedience; family respect; and sibling and peer rivalry. They are spiced with demons, ghosts, giants, demigods, and personified fish and animals. As William A. Lessa notes about Ulithian legends, they "...redefine reality so as to make the colorless colorful, the unknown knowable, and the intolerable tolerable." The spirits and monsters, however, were believed much more before the arrival of Christianity to the islands than after the missionary influence took hold. When actual belief in the supernatural in folktales was mitigated, much of the seriousness was lost, and with it the unquestioned belief in the stories.

Any study of the "literature" written by Micronesians in English must consider the fables, myths, legends and folklore of the area. Some of the following stories qualify for only one of these categories, while others encompass characteristics of several. Though they originated in widely scattered areas, they are alike in common motifs. The original purposes of folk stories were to inform, instruct, or amuse as mentioned earlier, and occasionally a selection would qualify for more than one of these purposes. Common topics are the origins of natural features, the peopling of islands, and the development of values, skills and social and political units. Encounters with spiritual beings and monsters are very frequent, as are animal and fish fables created for the entertainment of children.

Similar stories with local variations appear in tales about islands separated by languages and several thousand miles of Pacific Ocean. Thus we find islands in Palau, Yap, Truk and the Marshall Islands all being pulled apart by the power of monsters or giants. We see Ulithi, Gaferut, Pisiiras and Mwoakilloa all being raised from the ocean floor by human hands, and reefs at Namoluk, Nama, Satawan and Majuro all existing because of magical power. Often heroes (or rascals) reappear in a number of stories from a particular area. Truk has the female ghost Natuk and the mischievous, but lovable Olofat; Mwoakilloa has the lazy giant Lodup; and the Marshall Islands have the shrewd trickster Letao.

Some stories are quite lengthy in their entirety, and are often told in individual, semi-independent connecting segments. This is true particularly of tales from Yap, but connected tales also appear in the folklore of Truk and Pohnpei. Violence prevails throughout, but it is often the make-believe violence of childhood, and it is almost always the villainous who suffer.

The supernatural is alive and well in Micronesia and permeates its folktales. Verifiable historical fact is often combined with mythology in the same story. Americans and Europeans may differentiate between the historical as being real and factual and demons, monsters and spirits as being mythical. Not so the creators of folktales in the islands. Some stories with ghosts and demigods have the same claim to credibility as an historical event. The conquering of Pohnpei by Isokelekel and the building of Nan Madol are examples where bizarre and atypical characters and events blend with conventional local history. Time-dating and detail take leave of the stories, but events are nearly always logical and in a chronological sequence. Sizes and forms, however, frequently defy logic altogether. Detail is always lacking in the stories. A bird is simply a bird and not a noddy tern or a starling; "many years ago" and "long ago" may actually mean "formerly" or even "now." Generally, there is a division between simple tales told for amusement to children and those that are purportedly true, and this division is universal throughout Micronesian folk literature.

In all of the stories, morality prevails, and acceptable behavior and traits of character are exemplified so that they may be passed on from old to young, past to present, and hopefully from generation to generation.

# *Mokil or Mwoakilloa?*

E. H. Bryan Jr. in *Guide to Place Names in the Trust Territory of the Pacific Islands* (Honolulu, Pacific Science Center, Bernice P. Bishop Museum, 1971) lists twenty-seven different names or variations of spellings for Pohnpei Island alone. Many places in Micronesia have more than one name and most have several spellings. Where variations in names occur in the following pages, both the official and local spellings are listed below. In the first column are spellings accepted by the U.S. Board on Geographic Names and the island or atoll where the place name occurs. The local names and spellings appear in the second column. The names of archipelagos and main islands and atolls are those currently in use in the Western Pacific. Although a particular name may be mentioned in stories in subsequent chapters, it is only placed on the list under the chapter heading in which it initially appears.

Several islands or groups have officially changed names since Bryan's publication first appeared. Most notable, of course, is the change of the U.S. Trust Territory of the Pacific Islands to the four island entities of the Commonwealth of the Northern Mariana Islands, the Republic of Belau, the Federated States of Micronesia, and the Republic of the Marshall Islands. Other changes are Kusaie to Kosrae, Ponape to Pohnpei, Mokil to Mwoakilloa, and Ngatik Atoll to Sapwuahfik.

## Chapter I

| Official Place Name | Local Place Name |
|---|---|
| Palau | Belau |
| Yap Town | Colonia |
| Nif (Yap) | Kanifay |
| Iar (Ulithi) | Ear |
| Mangejang (Ulithi) | Magayang |
| Scheiben (Truk) | Pisiiras |
| Folo (Truk) | Fano |
| Ulalu (Truk) | Romonum |
| Onari (Namonuito) | Unanu |
| Weltot (Namonuito) | Weliot |
| Amas (Namoluk) | Ames |
| Sopuk (Truk) | Sapuk |
| Piasa (Lukunor) | Piafo |
| Ponape (Pohnpei) | Pohnpei |
| Nan Matol (Pohnpei) | Nan Madol |
| Langer (Pohnpei) | Langar |
| Mokil (Mwoakilloa) | Mwoakilloa |
| Mwanton (Mwoakilloa) | Mwandohn |
| Mokil Islet (Mwoakilloa) | Kahlap |
| Ngatik Atoll (Sapwuahfik) | Sapwuahfik |
| Peina (Sapwuahfik) | Paina |
| Tafonsak (Kosrae) | Tafunsak |
| Lele (Kosrae) | Lelu |
| Utwa (Kosrae) | Utwe |
| Malam (Kosrae) | Malem |
| Ebadon (Kwajalein) | Ebaten |

## Chapter II

| | |
|---|---|
| Ngarmid (Palau) | Ngermid |
| Rul (Yap) | Rull |
| Uatschaluk (Yap) | Fachaluk |
| Pata | Paata |
| Peniesene (Truk) | Peliesele |
| Mor (Satawan) | Moch |
| Mariong (Satawan) | Meriong |
| Kutu (Satawan) | Kattu |
| Jokaj (Pohnpei) | Sokehs |

*Chapter II* (continued)

| Official Place Name | Local Place Name |
|---|---|
| Sokehs Rock (Pohnpei) | Peipalap |
| Lod (Pohnpei) | Lohd |
| Metalanim (Pohnpei) | Madolenihmw |
| Not (Pohnpei) | Nett |
| Kiti (Pohnpei) | Kitti |
| Sukeru (Pingelap) | Sukoru |
| Walang (Kosrae) | Walung |
| Wakat (Kosrae) | Okat |

Chapter III

| | |
|---|---|
| Riquen (Yap) | Riken |
| Olimarao (Yap) | Olimari |
| Oneap (Satawan) | Oneop |
| Auak (Pohnpei) | Awak |
| Tolopuel (Pohnpei) | Dolopwail |
| Jelatak (Pohnpei) | Saladak |

# I.
# The Origins of Islands and Peoples

*Trukese Sailing Canoe*

*Uab of Palau*

# *Palau Islands*

## HOW THE ISLANDS OF PALAU WERE SEPARATED

The Palau Islands are separated by numerous channels and lagoons, but long ago, the islands are believed to have been one large land mass. How the land was broken into islands, and why people have different characteristics on the islands, is a story often told in Palau.

Today, the island of Angaur sits some five miles across the sea from its neighbor, Peleliu. It is believed, however, that Angaur and Peleliu were once a single piece of land. On the area of land there lived a very unusual man named Uab.

When Uab was only a child he would not play with other children, but was content to eat large amounts of food and to sleep. Even when he was very young he would eat much more food than adults, and so he grew to be enormous. As he got older, he ate more and more. Soon he was eating all of the food that his family could produce, and then he consumed all of the food of his neighbors as well. And he continued to grow larger and larger. Uab even had to move out of his house because it became too small for his huge body. Day by day, week by week, and year by year, Uab continued to grow. Finally, he was eating all of the food in the community and the people were starving, just to feed the ever-hungry Uab.

Uab's neighbors had to do something or they would all soon starve to death. They all met together and decided to burn the gigantic Uab and end their misery. So they built a large fire in a circle around the unsuspecting giant.

The fire raged around the giant, but Uab remained upright. At last he started to topple over. As he hit the ground he gave a violent kick with his enormous foot and pushed Peleliu far away from Angaur, where it remains today. The partly-submerged body of the fallen giant then formed islands. His legs became Koror, which has the most activity, and his penis became Aimeliik next to Koror, which today has the most rainy weather. The stomach of Uab formed Ngiwal, which is very rich in food crops, and his head rested at Ngerchelong, whose people are known for their intelligence.

And so it is today. The Palau Islands are separated, and different people have different characteristics, all because of the giant Uab who was burned and toppled, because he could not control his appetite.

# *Yap Islands*

## THE DAY THAT WAAB BECAME YAP

Long ago, before the arrival of foreigners on the islands of Yap, there lived two fishermen named Dan and Nang. They stayed on the northern end of the islands and were very good fishing companions. Whenever they returned from the sea, Dan and Nang would spend some time on the beach resting and dividing their catch between them, and then they went home.

One day while resting on the beach after fishing, a strange occurrence took place. They saw something large and white beyond the reef. At first they thought it was a moving island or a whale, since it was their first experience at seeing something so unusual. As they watched, a small boat detached itself from the object and moved toward Dan and Nang.

The fishermen waited as the small boat came closer to them, and it finally arrived near the shore. A man who was commanding the crew of the boat picked up his oar and held it high while shouting a question in English to Dan and Nang. The fishermen thought that the man was asking the name of the oar he was holding, and Dan and Nang responded *"yap,"* which is the word for oar in Yapese.

Today, the place name of Yap is widely known throughout the world because of this mistranslation. That is, everywhere except in the Yap Islands. There, the name *Waab* is used now, as it was used before the arrival of the strange visitors long ago.

## WHY SIPIN DISAPPEARED UNDER THE SEA

The people of Yap are known to be the most traditional in all of Micronesia. But even within Yap, some areas follow traditional ways more than others. At present, Rumung might be considered the most traditional, but not too long ago an island called Sipin had this distinction. Sipin disappeared one day without warning, and why this happened is known to many Yapese, but to few strangers.

Sipin Island was located to the east of Rumung Municipality. As some customs changed in other parts of Yap, those of Sipin remained the same. The people simply wanted to live as real Yapese without any interference from foreigners.

As more strangers began to arrive on Yap, the chief of Sipin saw that the old, reliable ways of his people were threatened. So he called a meeting one day to which all of the people of the island came. The chief explained the threat to their culture, and all of the people decided they did not want the foreign influence to invade their island. They told their neighbors on Rumung that they would find a way to keep the foreign customs away from Sipin, and asked if they would like to join with them. But the people of Rumung declined the offer.

At this time on Yap, people were half human and half ghosts, so the people of Sipin and their island were able to simply disappear from sight and sink below the surface of the sea. They did not sink down too far at first, though, as passing canoes could still see the island from the surface during daylight. They could also see the torches of the people of Sipin at night, and fishermen from Yap could hear the people below the surface talking, dancing, and working. As time passed, the island sank deeper into the sea, so at present the people of Sipin can no longer be heard or seen.

Fishermen from the main islands of Yap still search for the location of Sipin, because there are many fish in the area. When Sipin is found they always attach a rock to a float to mark the area so they can find the island when they return at another time. But when the fishermen return, their floats are always gone, as though someone beneath the surface was untying them and letting them drift away.

*Gaslew, Yapese Dance*

## HOW THE YAP ISLANDS BECAME SEPARATED

Centuries ago the municipalities of Rumung and Map in the Yap Islands were joined together, along with Gagil. Today, however, Yap consists of four separate islands with channels between them. The spaces between the islands were created by a fearful, monstrous sea-lizard, a *galuf*, that once lived in the lagoon of Yap.

A long time ago this lizard lived in an area called Mil, located where the three municipalities of Rumung, Map, and Fanif meet. He was extremely large and dangerous and would continually attack travelers who sailed on rafts and canoes. The lizard could swim faster than any canoe could move and so the people were restricted from traveling on water for fear of losing their lives.

Many brave men in Yap tried to trap or kill the lizard, but all failed. Finally, one young man named Pirow decided that to kill the lizard he would have to build a canoe that could sail faster than the lizard could swim, and then he would have to use a trick to kill the monster. So he set out on his task of constructing the fastest canoe on Yap.

To have the swiftest canoe, he knew that he must have a craft that could sail faster than a fish could be cooked. He built his first canoe of ironwood and launched it. Then he went fishing only long enough to catch a single fish. He gave the fish to his wife and instructed her to cook it on an open fire while he tested the speed of his canoe. When he returned home, he found that the fish was burned to ashes. This was a sure sign that his canoe was too slow to escape the lizard. And so another canoe was built, and another fish was caught and put on the fire by his wife. After testing the second canoe, the man returned to find the fish very nearly cooked, and so he knew his second canoe had not moved fast enough. And so he built a third canoe and repeated the process of putting a fish on the fire. When he returned

*Galuf* of Yap

from testing this third canoe, he found that the fish was still alive and struggling. He built five canoes. Then his sixth one was made from a breadfruit tree, and this craft was fast enough to escape the monster. He then went to the reef and found a very large clam which he attached to the outrigger of his canoe. The following day the man sailed into the Mil Channel. It was not long before the monster began to chase after the canoe. But the race was futile because the canoe sailed twice as fast as the lizard could swim. Finally the lizard begged the man to slow down so that he could rest because he was exhausted from swimming after the canoe. The man slowed his craft and then invited the lizard to climb onto the outrigger in order to rest for awhile. When the lizard saw the delicious clam he became his usual greedy self and put his ugly head into the shell to eat it. The shell immediately clamped shut, trapping the head of the monster inside.

The lizard struggled to free himself from the entrapment by swinging his tail viciously. The tail hit Rumung and Map, separating these islands. Then it hig Gagil, and separated it from Map with a channel that is often used today.

These events happened centuries ago, and the separation of the islands of Yap is evidence that these events really took place.

## HOW YAP BECAME POPULATED

Once there were only a few people on Yap and traditions were strictly enforced. This was especially true of commands made by the chief. The whole island obeyed only one leader and the population was a mixture of people and ghosts.

The one great chief, Rugog, lived at a place which is still known as a high caste village. This place is called Teb. One time the chief heard about a beautiful lady who was a ghost and stayed on a stone outside the village, but the people could not catch her. Each time that they would try, she would escape under the stone.

The chief brought together all of his workers and slaves to try to find out how the beautiful lady ghost could be captured. It happened that there was a man in the group who had his eyes in back of his head—when he was going backward, he appeared to be going forward. A plan was made to fly kites to distract the lady, and then the man would walk up and capture her with a net, while seeming to be walking in the opposite direction. The plan worked, and the beautiful lady was taken prisoner. She was then brought to the chief.

The lady's name was Leebirang, and they were soon married. But Leebirang became very lonely in the new place and so her mother came to visit her. All of the people of Tomil were told by the chief to feed the mother, who had a very great appetite. So all of the people provided her with food. Soon, however, the people got tired of feeding the mother because she ate too much. The mother then had to steal sugarcane from the chief's garden. When the chief found that his sugarcane was disappearing, he set a trap and the mother was caught in it. This caused a great typhoon to hit the island with seas so high that all of the people were washed away except for Leebirang and Rugog.

The chief and his lady ghost wife eventually had seven sons and they were distributed among the seven municipalities of Yap. This is how the islands again became populated. The youngest son was given the chief's place and Teb remains a high-caste village to this day. In the 18th century, the chief's grave was dug up to find out how tall he had been. He measured seven feet and some inches, the tallest among Micronesians. A dance was composed for him that is still performed on Yap today.

*Leebirang of Yap*

## HOW A PART OF YAP WAS CLAIMED BY A TRICK

Gilman Municipality is now connected to Kanifay in the southern part of Yap, but for awhile it was separated. This was at the time of the *Davine Bol*, the great typhoon and tidal wave that swept over Yap and spared only Chief Rugog and his wife, Leebirang. Gilman was swept away, and a trick was used to claim the land by a man from the island of Tomil.

After the great typhoon and tidal wave, the islands slowly and gradually became repopulated by these two survivors. During the great typhoon, however, Gilman disappeared and it was unclaimed by anyone.

One day a young man from Gagil sailed off to the south and found Gilman. He claimed it for himself and his ancestors and he left a fresh, green branch from a tree stuck into the ground to show his mark of ownership. Some time passed, and a man from Tomil also happened upon Gilman. Although he saw the mark of the previous visitor, he refused to acknowledge that the island was not his own. So he found a very old, weathered branch with nearly rotten leaves and he stuck it in the earth as his mark of possession.

Stories of the drifted-away and rediscovered land spread throughout Gagil and Tomil. Naturally, when both men claimed the land, a dispute arose. Both men claimed to have left a branch stuck in the ground and both said this proved ownership. The first man, from Gagil, had placed a fresh green branch. However, the second man, from Tomil, had placed an old rotting branch. Since the branch of the second visitor was obviously older, it was decided that he must have been the first to arrive. Therefore, the people agreed that the person from Tomil should win the dispute.

Today it is still recalled in Yap how Gilman was won by a man from Tomil Tomil who tricked a man from Gagil with an old and rotten branch. The incident is further remembered by the name, Gilman, which in Yapese means the drifted-away part of Gagil.

# *Yap Outliers*

## HOW ULITHI WAS FORMED

There is a legend told on Ulithi about how Mogmog became the main islet in the atoll. The story is about a woman, Felta, who was unhappy with her two selfish brothers and left her home on Yap by using magic powers.

Long ago, the islands of Ulithi did not exist, and Felta lived on Yap with her two brothers. She was older than her brothers and she was very wise in many ways. Her younger brothers, however, did not treat her kindly. Every day when they caught turtles, they would only give Felta the least desirable parts such as the heads and fins. This made Felta very unhappy and hurt.

One day she decided to leave Yap because of the unkind treatment from her brothers. Felta walked away from home, but when she reached the beach she could go no further because of the ocean beyond. So she took a coconut shell and filled it with sand and walked toward the water. Then she said some magic words and threw some of the sand into the sea. Suddenly this sand formed a long and narrow sandbar, and Felta walked on it until she reached the end. She then said some magic words and threw more sand into the sea. This caused another sandbar to form and she again walked on it until she reached its end. Felta kept doing this over and over again until she came to where Ulithi is today. And there she decided to stay. She built all of the islets on the atoll and chose Ear as her first home.

One day Felta built a fire, and its drifting smoke pointed toward the islet of Mangayang. So she decided to move there. Before long, however, Felta moved again, because there were too many rats on Mangayang. This time she moved to the islet of Mogmog. Felta was very happy on Mogmog because she could see most of Ulithi from there. She made Mogmog her permanent home and cultivated many different plants on the island. Also, there were a lot of turtles on

Mogmog and she could eat any parts of them that she desired without worrying about her selfish brothers.

While staying on Mogmog, Felta gave birth to a son. She named the boy Lorob. Felta taught Lorob many useful skills such as how to build houses and canoes. When Lorob grew up, Felta sent him to Yap to bring coconut plants back to Ulithi as there were no coconuts on the atoll at that time.

Today, Ulithi is covered with coconut trees and the atoll has very many islets because of Felta and her son Lorob. Mogmog is also the main islet in the atoll because it was the final home of Felta, the woman who formed Ulithi.

## THE DISCOVERY OF AN UNDERSEA ISLAND

The people of Ulithi believe that there is a mysterious island deep under the sea where men live and work. This island was found by one of two brothers who lived on the islet of Lam in Ulithi Atoll long ago.

One of the brothers was sane and normal and the other brother was crazy and unpredictable. People did not understand the mad brother and were very much afraid of him because they never knew what he would do next. He bothered the people of Lam so much that his sane brother was ashamed of him.

One day the sane brother realized that he must be rid of his crazy brother for the good of the community. So he took his brother fishing, and they sailed their canoe far out into the open sea. At a great distance from Ulithi, the normal brother tied a large stone around the neck of his mad brother, and then threw him overboard to drown. Then he sailed sadly back to his home.

A month passed, and the brother went out alone on the reef to fish. Suddenly, he heard someone calling his name in a familiar voice. When he looked around, he saw his drowned brother walking toward him. He was startled, and so afraid that he tried to run away. But his crazy brother called after him to wait because there were things he had to tell him. When the sane brother realized that his brother was no longer crazy, he stopped and they walked back to Lam together.

The brother who had been drowned told a strange story of sinking to an island under the sea. There he found houses and men working. These men had accepted him and treated him kindly. They taught him new methods of making ropes and different ways of fishing. Since the men did not know he was insane, they did not treat him like a crazy man. So the brother forgot he was crazy and became normal again.

The formerly-insane brother returned to Ulithi, showed the people what he had learned, and told them all about the undersea island. Today, many people on the island believe that there is a secret place under the sea near Ulithi that was discovered by a crazy brother.

## WHY FASU DISAPPEARED FROM IFALIK

At one time there was a large island with a high mountain to the east of Ifalik in the outer islands of Yap State. But the island and the mountain have disappeared, and this was caused by magic used accidentally by Yapese visitors to the atoll.

*Fasu near Ifalik*

It happened that a sailing canoe arrived at Ifalik from Yap. The people of Ifalik welcomed the navigator and his crew, as is the custom, and young girls brought flowered wreaths, *nunuws,* to the strangers.

The visitors were guided to a comfortable canoe house and they were invited by the chief to stay there as long as they wished. However, the chief would not permit the Yapese to leave the area of the canoe house and move around Ifalik. The chief was well aware that many Yapese possessed powerful magic and he did not want this potential danger spread around Ifalik.

Early one morning, the Yapese navigator sneaked away from the canoe house and went to the eastern side of Ifalik to bathe. He cut a coconut in half and used the oil for his soap. He then ground the coconut meat with a small clam shell and placed it on a leaf on the beach. Then he leaped into the sea to swim around a bit. Suddenly he saw something strange on the horizon, although the bright morning sun made it difficult for the navigator to see clearly. The apparition looked fearful in the dawn light and the navigator was convinced he was seeing a great typhoon brewing in the east. So he immediately swam ashore and ran inland. Then he collected leaves and other ingredients known only to magicians and returned to the shoreline. When all was ready, he said some magic words, and the fearful object disappeared.

A few moments later, the navigator went to tell the chief that he had prevented a typhoon from striking the island by using magic. The chief was startled, and told the navigator that it was not a typhoon that he had eliminated, but an island with a large mountain, thinking it was a typhoon. The navigator apologized profusely to the chief for his mistake. The chief accepted the apology, but then told the Yapese to leave Ifalik immediately.

The area is known locally as Fasu, and today only an outline of the island that disappeared, barely submerged under the sea northeast of Ifalik remains. Ships avoid the area, but men often fish there when the winds from the east assure an easy return to Ifalik. What was once a high island is now an area whose permanent residents are fish, and all because of magic misused by a Yapese navigator who did not obey the wishes of the chief.

## HOW GAFERUT WAS RAISED FROM THE SEA

The tiny island of Gaferut in the outer islands of Yap State sits alone some distance from the nearest neighboring island. It is believed that this island was formed by an unhappy lady who left Ifalik with her young daughter and her niece.

This lady lived on Ifalik with her older sister. Both of the sisters had young daughters. One day the younger sister asked the older one to look after her child while she went to the taro patch to gather food for all of them. Before leaving, however, she instructed the older sister to bathe her baby in her own tub if the child cried, and not in the tub belonging to her niece.

While the young sister was gathering food, her baby cried. The older sister felt that it would be too much trouble to bathe the child in its own tub, so she simply put the baby in the tub of her child instead. When this happened, however, the younger sister felt it immediately, as she was possessed with magic powers. Since her older sister was so careless and had completely ignored her request, the younger sister decided to leave Ifalik forever. She returned early from the taro patch and asked her sister to cook the food. While the older sister was occupied with cleaning the taro, she took her baby and her sister's child and sneaked away from the house.

With her magic powers, she headed north toward Faraulep. There she gathered particular grasses for a magic potion, filled a cup with sand, and went to a rock on the reef of Faraulep. There she prepared her secret mixture. As she traveled further and further, she listened for the sound of waves striking the island. Finally, when she could hear no sound of the surf, she emptied her cup of sand, dropped her potion, and uttered magic words. This caused a small island to surface from the sea, and there she decided to live with the two children.

And so the trip that started on Ifalik ended with an island called Gaferut being raised from the sea, but the important magic medicine was made from grasses found on Faraulep. And the rock remains on the reef of Faraulep today, with grasses still growing prominently. Despite waves and rough seas that sometimes cover this rock completely, the grasses refuse to be torn away by the ocean.

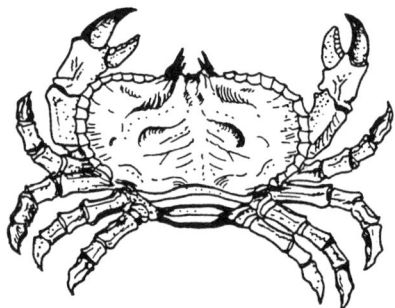

Much later, the people of Faraulep discovered the island accidentally. As they approached Gaferut, the lady changed the children into a bird and a fish, and she changed herself into a crab. And that is all that the voyagers from Faraulep found on Gaferut. The island remains uninhabited, except for these creatures, to this day.

# Truk Islands

## HOW A MOUNTAIN ON TOL BECAME ISLETS

There is a large number of small islets around the three big islands of Tol in Truk Lagoon. A story is told about how the small islands were formed by a woman and her brother from the larger islands on Tol.

Akapitto and his sister Niepanung lived on two different mountains. One day they decided to compete to see who could build a mountain to be the highest. Early in the morning the race began. They each piled up rocks and soil as fast as they could throughout the day. By nightfall, the sister Niepanung had beaten her brother Akapitto in the contest.

Being beaten by his sister caused Akapitto to be very angry, and he was determined to defeat his sister in a second contest. So he challenged her to see who could reduce their mountain to the ground the fastest. Niepanung was a very wise woman, and so she thought of a way to once again beat her angry brother.

When the contest started, Niepanung was the first to attack her mountain. She only kicked the top of it off, though, and the piece flew into the sea and became the small islet of Onang. Seeing this, Akapitto raged and shouted again and again as his sister watched. Other islets were formed as Akapitto kicked his mountain into islets until it was flat.

From that time on, Tol has had many small islands near the three main ones. Also, this is the reason why the mountain of Niepanung is the highest of all of those on Tol to this day.

## HOW PISIIRAS WAS RAISED FROM THE SEA

On the island of Moen in Truk Lagoon there once lived five brothers. Before their parents died, their father called all of the boys together to talk to them. He told his sons of a lost island near Moen and said that some day they should search for it.

A few years after their father died, the five brothers set sail in search of the lost island. For three days they searched the waters hoping to find it. On the fourth day they returned disheartened to Moen. Four of the five brothers decided that their father had fooled them them with his story, but the fifth brother, the youngest, still believed that his father had told the truth.

So the youngest son again set sail, without his brothers, in search of the island. After traveling a short distance, he saw that a huge shark was guiding his sailing canoe. The shark was so willing to lead the canoe that the boy thought that the fish must be the ghost of his dead father. The shark swam with the canoe until they reached the area of the lost island, and then the shark vanished from sight.

The youngest son lowered his sails and dropped his anchor. Then he dived deeply below the surface of the sea and found the lost island. When he returned to the surface and boarded his canoe, he tried to raise his anchor, but found that it was stuck. He pulled and pulled with all of his strength, but he could not budge it. So finally he cut his anchor rope and sailed back to his home on Moen.

When he returned, the younger brother told the others what he had seen. Early the next day all five of the sons sailed off to find the island. When they arrived at the area, the oldest brother dove into the water and tied a rope to the island. After returning to the boat he pulled on the rope but the island could not be raised from the bottom. Then the second brother tried, but even with all his strength he could not move the island. Then the third brother tried to raise the island and then the fourth brother, but the result was the same—the island could not be raised from the ocean floor. The youngest brother then tugged on the rope and the island amazingly came up to the surface. At that very moment, a black bird flew overhead and called to the boys. The bird told the brothers that the island should be called

Pisiiras and must forever remain the property of the youngest son who believed his father.

About a mile north of Moen sits a small island all by itself. There, descendants of the younger brother still live, and the island is still called Pisiiras, the name of the clan of the brothers.

## WHY FANO SPLIT AWAY FROM MOEN

Long ago there were thirteen villages on Moen. The people of Fano were upset at the time because they did not have enough food. Their protector god, Lupoponumong, was always away, and as a result, spirits from other villages came and stole their food. The people of Fano were starving. Some of them only survived on water that came out of a large rock in their village. When Lupoponumong finally returned to Fano, the god was very upset at the other villages for their treatment of the Fano people, and a curse was put upon them. The Fano spirit said that all of the villages would be dry and without drinking water. When this happened after a short time, the people and the gods from other villages swarmed to Fano to get water from the well-known rock. Lupoponumong, though, refused to give away the water. So the gods of the other villages got together and attacked Lupoponumong. To escape the attack, Lupoponumong picked up the land on which the village stood and cast it into the lagoon, a mile away from Moen.

Today, the previous location of Fano on Moen is a large indented body of water like a bay. In 1980, a bridge was put up over it to connect the villages on either side. From the air one can see that Fano would fit snugly in the inlet between Tunuk and Mechitiu where it once was located. And the rock from which the water flows is still there. It is called *Aparo*, which means hidden water.

## HOW AN ISLET WAS PUSHED AWAY FROM UDOT

There is a small island just offshore from Udot in the Truk Lagoon. This piece of land was pushed away from the main island by a sad Yapese lady who lost her magic when she disobeyed her father.

Nemwes was the name of the unusual lady from Yap. She was fully twelve feet tall, very slender, and her parents were the most renowned magicians on Yap. Her greatest enjoyment was gathering flowers with which she made the most lovely *mwaramwars*.

A time came when Nemwes had used nearly all of the flowers in Yap. So she asked her parents if she could travel to Truk to gather more flowers. At first her parents refused permission, but since Nemwes insisted, her parents finally consented to let her go. They loved her dearly, and did not want to disappoint her. Her father, though, warned his daughter that she must not visit the island of Udot to take flowers. He said that she could visit any island in Truk, but if she went to Udot, her magic would be useless. He also warned her that if she set foot on Udot, she would never get away to return home.

Nemwes left early the next morning. Her powerful magic allowed her to walk on the sea, so a canoe was not necessary. When she reached Truk she gathered flowers on many islands and came closer and closer to Udot. When the chief of Udot spied Nemwes from his vantage point on the top of a hill, he ordered his men to invite her to the island. The men were amazed to find she was so tall and slender. Since Nemwes was curious about Udot, she ignored the advice of her father and went to the meeting house of the chief when she was invited on the island.

The chief of Udot entertained Nemwes royally and provided her with the best food and drink. But Nemwes did not know that a potion had been slipped into her food that made her own magic useless. When she left, she gathered more flowers and walked toward the sea.

Nemwes stepped onto the water and her foot immediately sank to the bottom. She then stepped backwards, took her most potent magic from her basket, and tried again. But her foot sank to the bottom a second time. She then realized that she could no longer walk home and that she must remain on Udot forever. Nemwes sat on the beach and cried and wailed. In her misery, she kicked her long legs outward, and a small island was formed to the south of the larger island. This island remains where Nemwes pushed it to this very day.

The parents of Nemwes tried to find her. First they sent a turtle to search for her. The turtle swam directly to Udot, but the people caught it, killed it, and ate the meat. They then sent the shell back to Yap. Since Nemwes did not return with the shell, the parents knew that they would never see their daughter again. But they made one further attempt to find her by sending a large fish to Udot. The people caught it, though, ate it without breaking any of its bones, and by magic sent the skeleton back to Yap.

The small beautiful island kicked away from Udot by Nemwes remains off the island today, and is known for its great variety of

beautiful flowers. Also, if one visits the small island, one will find a cave that is twelve feet high, the exact height of the girl, and a large rock resembling a woman sitting, with flowing hair, as a reminder of the sad story of Nemwes.

## WHY A PART OF UMAN WAS MOVED TO MURILO

At one time in the Truk Islands, Uman had a small, uninhabited island located near to it. This island was used by the people of Uman for growing tobacco and it contained very rich soil for this purpose.

One day the chief of the Hall Islands called a meeting of all his people. At that time, the men had to sail great distances to get tobacco because it would not grow on their islands. The chief told his people that he would solve the problem by taking an island next to Uman and bringing it all the way to Murilo. Although the chief was highly respected, the people doubted that it would be possible to move an entire island.

Time passed and the people nearly forgot the chief's promise to move an island. The chief grew to be very old. Shortly before he died he called for his elder son to come to him. The old chief taught his son all that he knew about the traditional ways of his people, and also taught the son about magic. Soon afterward, the chief died and the son assumed his position, as this was the custom in the Hall Islands.

The new chief never forgot what his father had said about the island next to Uman, and he decided to use the magic that his father had taught him to bring the island to his people. So one day he boarded his canoe and sailed all the way to Truk Lagoon. The dead chief had advised his son what to do when entering the islands of Truk, and the son remembered well what his father had told him. He had been told not to stop or to speak to anyone, but to sail on until he reached the small island next to Uman.

It was morning when he arrived at his destination. He went directly to the center of the island and performed the secret magic that was only known to chiefs. Then the island began to move, but very slowly at first. Then more magic was performed and the island moved faster and faster. The people of Uman were terrified as they saw the small island move away from them. They thought that it must be a god moving the island and not a man performing magic. The island moved all the way out of Truk Lagoon and settled far to the north in the Hall Islands.

Today this islet sits between Ruo and Murilo islets. It has very rich soil and is unlike any of those surrounding it. And to this day, the people of the Hall Islands use this strange, imported islet for growing their tobacco.

## HOW UNANU BECAME POPULATED

There is an islet in Namonuito Atoll in the Western Islands of Truk State with the unique name locally of Unanu. The meaning of the name is daughters of the ghost, and an interesting story is known throughout the Western Islands about how this place was named.

Many years ago Unanu was unnamed and uninhabited. At that time a group of ghosts had been migrating from place to place in the Western Islands in search of a home where they could permanently settle. The ghosts finally came upon this deserted island, they liked it, and they decided to remain there.

As the years passed, it became known to all of the people in the Western Islands that this particular place was inhabited by ghosts. Consequently, islanders from other atolls in the area feared visiting the ghosts' island.

A man named Olofat happened to be living on a nearby island called Weliot. He was very clever and curious, and decided to investigate the fearful island of the ghosts. So one night he left on his voyage and planned to arrive at his destination during daylight when all ghosts are known to be sleeping. When he arrived there, he walked quietly past the homes of the ghosts until he came to the house of the chief. There, Olofat was startled to see the most beautiful ghost-lady imaginable sleeping on her mat. She was the daughter of the chief of the ghosts. Olofat carefully and patiently awakened the girl and talked to her. And almost immediately Olofat and the beautiful ghost-lady fell in love with each other.

*Trukese Love Sticks*

Olofat and his ghost-mistress decided to leave the island at once because they knew that the chief ghost would object to their being together. So they sailed to Weliot where they could live happily together. That night, after the ghosts had awakened, they discovered that the chief's daughter was gone. They realized that someone had taken her away, so they began a search of all the islands in the area.

The ghosts searched throughout all of the Western Islands, but they were unable to find the missing girl. It happened that Olofat possessed magical powers. When a searcher would come near his island, Olofat would turn the island upside down in the ocean so that it could not be seen. When the danger had passed, Olofat would then turn the island right-side up again.

For two years the lovers stayed together in the seclusion of Olofat's island. Eventually, though, the girl became pregnant and asked to return to her island to be with her people when she gave birth. But when they arrived at her home, they found the island to be deserted because the other ghosts were still out searching for the girl.

Soon Olofat's wife delivered twin girls. They named their daughters Un and Anu. The girls grew up and became the first people to permanently settle the island. And today, on any map of Namonuito Atoll, Unanu is clearly visible in the east as a reminder of Olofat, his wife, and the daughters of the ghost.

# *Truk Outliers*

### THE GHOST-WOMAN OF NOMWIN

Long ago, the people of Nomwin were happy, contented, and carefree. They were healthy, and food and fresh water were plentiful. Then one day a ghost nearly destroyed the island and its people by taking away their food, wildlife, and water.

On the far side of the island a ghost-woman lived under a large rock. She would hide during the day, but would often come out at night and sneak around where people were feasting, drinking, dancing, talking and clapping. Night was a very special time for the men and women of Nomwin, especially the young people. The female ghost would steal some food when the people were distracted, and then return to her home under the rock before daybreak.

One day the chief ordered all of the men to go fishing and for each to bring back ten fish. He also sent all of the women into the bush and told them to return with a basket of food each. That night, an extra big feast was given and everyone was enjoying the party. The chief's son attended with the girl he was to marry, the most beautiful of all the young girls on Nomwin.

The night after the party, the girl to whom the chief's son was engaged was bathing by the seashore. Suddenly the ghost-woman appeared. Her face was shining like the sun and her eyes were like fire. The ghost seized the poor, frightened girl and held her under the water. Her skirt and flowered lei were all that floated to the surface as the beautiful girl drowned.

When people came to the shore, they found the body of the unfortunate girl. The entire island went into mourning. Then the chief commanded all of the men to search for the killer of his son's betrothed wife. Footprints, much larger than any human's, were in the sand and the men followed them to the ghost-woman. When she saw the approaching party, she became angry and fled to a nearby islet. She hated the people for tracking her, and so that night she returned and took away all of the food on Nomwin. She even took the birds away from the island, and all of the wells dried up because she also took away the water. Older people and children were dying of starvation and from thirst and the people knew that they must make peace with the cruel ghost-woman.

First they attempted to give tribute to the ghost by offering her the little food that they had left, but she refused to accept it. Then they tried to appease the ghost with entertainment. They gathered the best and most beautiful dancers of Nomwin at the shore opposite the ghost's island and had them perform for her. The ghost-woman was so thrilled with the dances that she threw bunch after bunch of food to the dancers and it floated around Nomwin. Then she returned the water to Nomwin by bringing it to the island in her throat. At the shoreline she opened her mouth and the water poured out into the sand.

If one visits the atoll at present, the food thrown by the ghost-woman can still be seen. It now appears as individual small islets scattered near the main island and they are rich in food crops. The place where the girl was killed is still seen as a shape of a naked woman on the beach. It has since been turned into stone. And whenever one is thirsty while walking along the shore, it is only necessary to dig in the sand to find pure drinking water left by the ghost-woman a long time ago.

*Trukese Devil Mask*

## HOW LUKUNOR BECAME POPULATED

At one time a small group of people from Sapuk village on Moen went fishing far away on the barrier reef south of the island. In the party were three men and two women. As the group headed homeward at the end of the day, a terrible storm suddenly struck them. In the confusion, the group was scattered and all were lost except for one of the women.

The lone survivor was saved by a bundle of copra that had been on the boat. She held onto it and floated for days. It happened that the woman was pregnant at the time. Then she felt coral beneath her feet and shouted, *Och Nuku*," meaning, Oh! It's a reef. And this is the origin of the name of Lukunor Island which in Trukese is *Lukun-och*.

There were only a few coconut trees lining the shore when the woman was cast up on Lukunor's beach. She gathered fronds from the coconut palms and made a shelter. She was able to survive on the food from sea shells and coconut fruit and liquid. Time passed and finally she was ready to deliver. She gave birth to twin boys.

One day a canoe from Ettal was passing and saw signs of life on the island. When the canoe landed, the two young boys and the mother appeared. The leader of the group listened to the woman's story and was so impressed with her qualities that he decided to marry her. Many of the people of Lukunor have their origins from this couple who lived long, long ago.

## WHY PIAFO WAS MOVED TO LUKUNOR

Among the skills practiced by the people of Lukunor Atoll in the Mortlock Islands, navigation is one of the most important. There is a story about how navigation was taught by a father to his son. This story also explains how an islet of Losap Atoll was mysteriously moved to Lukunor.

In the past, and even today, navigators from Lukunor were known throughout the Mortlock Islands. Among the best navigators was a man named Anoun Foeng. He had one son named Sou Foeng who loved to practice navigation with his father.

One day Anoun Foeng told his son to prepare for a voyage to Moen Island in Truk Lagoon. The real purpose of the voyage was to test Sou Foeng's skills of navigation. They sailed to distant Moen as Anoun Foeng taught his son all that the boy could absorb about navigation. After arriving on Moen, the father felt that his son knew enough to plot his own way back to Lukunor.

After some time on Moen, Anoun Foeng took Sou Foeng to the seashore one morning. They went to inspect the weather. As they watched the sunrise, the exact day of departure was determined. When this day arrived, the return voyage to Lukunor was begun.

Sou Foeng plotted the course and led the voyage, assisted by his father. The first destination enroute was Losap Atoll in the Upper Mortlock Islands. Losap was the second largest islet in the lagoon and Piafo was next in size. Piafo was particularly beautiful with many coconut and mountain apple trees. It also had a nice long sandy beach.

When they reached Losap Atoll, they paused for several days on Piafo. The boy, Sou Foeng, loved the island but soon it was time to resume their voyage. Sou Foeng did not want to leave this beautiful place. He cried and pleaded with his father to stay. Since the journey could not be resumed without Sou Foeng, his father made him a promise. Anoun Foeng promised that the island would belong to his son when they arrived on Lukunor. The boy knew that a promise to a first-born son was respected and always kept, so he believed his father and the voyage was continued.

Anoun Foeng possessed a powerful magic called *Ngorongorin Faneu*. He whispered some magic words and Piafo was moved from the reef on Losap to the reef on Lukunor. When Sou Foeng reached home, Piafo was already resting on the reef of Lukunor. Sou Foeng was elated at the sight of the beautiful Piafo at Lukunor Atoll.

The former location of Piafo can still be seen on the reef of Losap Atoll and the roots of the coconut and apple trees are still there. The lovely island of Piafo, with its long sandy beach and rich vegetation, is now a part of Lukunor because of Anoun Foeng's promise to his son.

## HOW THE ISLETS OF ETTAL WERE FORMED

A story is known throughout the Lower Mortlocks about how the atolls were created by a turtle and an unusual fish. Ettal Atoll is isolated, has only one main inhabited islet, and a different physical shape than neighboring Lukunor Atoll to the east and Satawan Atoll to the south. This resulted from a plan by the turtle, Pwapwa, and a mischievous fish, Lippar, who would not follow instructions.

Long ago the fish and the turtle were very good friends. At that time there were no islands in the Lower Mortlocks and the two just swam together in the vast ocean a great distance from Truk Lagoon in the north. One day Pwapwa decided to form some atolls where the Lower Mortlocks are today, and he asked Lippar for help. They agreed to work at the same time building different islets, and Pwapwa asked Lippar to work on Ettal while Pwapwa worked separately on the atolls of Lukunor and Satawan. Pwapwa told his friend that the main islets should be facing each other and not isolated. There should be a circular lagoon and the islands should have a large coral reef connecting them.

Pwapwa worked hard on the atolls of Lukunor and Satawan,

and he built the main islets such as Oneop, Ta, Kuttu, and of course, the islets of Satawan and Lukunor also. These islets he connected with long circular reefs to make them accessible. Lippar, however, had a mind of his own and he was naturally mischievous. He built Ettal away from the others and even built it facing a different direction. He added no main islets such as Moch, Ta, and Kuttu on Satawan Atoll or Oneop on Lukunor Atoll, and he even built the atoll semi-circular, rather than circular as he had been told to.

After completing work on the atolls of Lukunor and Satawan, Pwapwa swam to see how his good friend was progressing. When he saw what Lippar had built—an islet isolated from others, the atoll facing a different direction, and having a strange shape—he was immediately angry. He corrected Lippar, but the fish only laughed at the turtle's anger. And the more furious Pwapwa became, the more Lippar antagonized him by laughing. Finally the turtle became so angry that he stepped as hard as he could right on top of the fish, flattening him and caused both eyes to be on one side of his body.

The atolls of Satawan, Lukunor, and Ettal have their shapes, islets and positions because of the work of these two creatures so many years ago. If one visits Ettal one would find an unusual fish that hides in the sand on sea bottoms. He is flat in shape, and his two eyes appear to be on one side of his body. This was caused by the anger of Pwapwa when he stepped on Lippar so many years ago.

## *Pohnpei Island*

### THE ORIGINS OF POHNPEI

There are many versions of stories told about the origin of Pohnpei Island. The following one is probably the best known. There are many essentials on the island today. Among these are coral, rocks, mangrove trees, fertile soil, palms, and huts. How these came to be is told in a popular story about the formation of Pohnpei.

Many years ago on a small island lived a man named Sapwkini. He was very skilled and so he built a large canoe with which to sail off into the unknown. He asked a number of other people to accompany him, and so with men, women, and children. Sapwkini set sail. The group traveled a great distance and then they came upon an octopus in mid-ocean named Lidakika. Sapwkini asked the creature from where he had come, and the octopus answered that his home was in the shallow water to the south. So Sapwkini and his group steered the canoe southward, and after sailing for some distance, they arrived at the home of the octopus. There they found a small piece of coral protruding from the sea and decided to build an island.

*Octopus Lidakika and Sapwkini*

Sapwkini and his followers began adding rocks and coral, but the waves always washed them away. Finally they added mangrove trees to the spot to hold the land in place. From that time onward, mangrove trees in Pohnpeian have been called keepers of the shore. Then a large barrier reef was added, and finally a *pei,* or altar was constructed where the gods could be worshipped.

When the new island was formed, all of the people left except for a single couple. In the years that followed, this man and woman had numerous children and the new land gradually increased its population. Other groups came to inhabit the new island and to add to its development. One group was led by Konapwel which means soil in Pohnpeian, and they helped the land to be fertile. Another group came bringing many different foods, and these were also the first individuals to construct huts. An additional group arrived bringing ivory-nut palms, the material used for making thatch roofing for homes.

According to popular legend, these groups were the first to populate Pohnpei, and bring the necessities of life to the island. And all things that are native to the island have their origins from these four groups of people who came to Pohnpei long ago.

## THE DEMIGOD BUILDERS OF NAN MADOL

Olsihpa and Olsohpa were two brothers who came to Pohnpei from the west. Both had magical powers which helped them to construct the famous artificial islands and settlements known as Nan Madol. At the time of the brothers' arrival on Pohnpei, the island was ruled by many clan leaders who were always fighting. The brothers wanted to unite the people under a single ruler and build a place for worship of the gods.

At first Olsihpa and Olsohpa were not successful in their building efforts. They started at Sokehs, but gave up and moved to Nett. The second site was also unsuitable and the brothers moved eastward into U. This place was also unsuitable and they finally found an area of Madolenihmw where a stone stairway seemed to lead to an underwater city known to be occupied by gods. Here they made a fourth attempt to build their settlement. Because the brothers were demigods, all of the people of the island volunteered to help. Nan Madol would be built in shallow water for protection, and also to be near the eel Nan Somohl, the earth figure of a god in heaven. It would be the spiritual center for all of the people of Pohnpei.

A center stone named Pehirahni was initially erected around which Nan Madol would be built. The sea continually washed away the construction efforts and so large basalt rocks with magical qualities were flown over the mountains of Pohnpei to the site. Other large stones were rafted long distances from stone quarries across the island. The work went on and on, some say for more than a hundred years.

When the islets were nearly completed, Olsihpa died, even though he was able to live longer than most people because of his magic. Finally, ninety-three basalt and coral islands were finished. Half of the islets were used as a religious center and the other half as a residence for nobility and priests.

The last builder of Nan Madol, Olsohpa, died when the project was completed. Before his death, however, he united the clan chiefs under a single ruler called the *Saudeleur* who resided at the spiritual center of Nan Madol called Pahn Kedira.

*Nan Madol Ruins*

## HOW LANGAR WAS FORMED

Langar Island in Pohnpei's lagoon is very much like the main island. It rests on firm basaltic rock, it has a high hill, fertile soil and lush vegetation just like Pohnpei. It even has a fringe reef surrounding it. Once, however, Langar was completely flat. A woman named Li en Lan was responsible for making Langar the way we see it today.

At one time, such a drenching rainfall occurred that nearly all of Pohnpei was washed away. The flooding waters caused a strong current to form and trees, bushes, rocks and houses were swept away into the sea. On Langar at the time lived the woman Li en Lan. When she saw everything from Pohnpei being washed away, she climbed to the top of a large rock. From there, she grabbed everything she could as the debris washed past Langar. She piled it all on her islet until the flood was over and the water receded. When she stopped working, she looked around to see that she had created a lovely high islet with a small mountain and bushes and soil and trees that had all of the characteristics of Pohnpei. Langar has remained this way ever since.

# *Pohnpei Outliers*

## HOW MWOAKILLOA WAS RAISED FROM THE SEA

The atoll of Mwoakilloa has three islets with unusual names and different characteristics. Three brothers long ago were responsible for these different characteristics, and for finding and naming the islets. Also, the three brothers and their mother were responsible for the coconut palm trees so prevalent on Mwoakilloa today.

The three brothers were named Ur, Mwa, and Ka. Ur was the firstborn son, Mwa was the next born, and Ka was the youngest. When these three boys were growing up their parents provided everything for them. The boys were also taught very practical skills by their mother and father. They were trained to dig and plant taro in patches, to climb trees in order to collect coconuts and breadfruit, and to build fine canoes. They also learned how to fish. The three boys were not equally good in all of these skills, however. Although Ur and Mwa could grow crops to support themselves, they were not the best farmers. Ka was the best farmer, but was the poorest fisherman of the three.

When they all went fishing together, Ka, the youngest, had difficulty catching fish for himself. His brothers laughed and made fun of him because they were better fishermen. Sometimes Ka would ask his older brothers to let him use their fish hooks, but this only made them laugh more. Only when the older brothers had a bad hook would they give it to Ka. When he used the hook, it would tangle on a rock continually, and Ur and Mwa would laugh even more.

On one particular day all of the brothers went fishing together in the same canoe. The hook of Ka again got tangled and the others laughed as usual and teased him. Ka then pulled hard, but the hook would not budge. Then the younger brother pulled and tugged as hard as he possibly could. When he felt something move, all of the brothers realized that an unusual occurrence was happening. Ka kept pulling on his fishing line even harder. At last, an island was pulled to the surface, and it consisted of three islets.

The three brothers were very happy at this unusual surprise. Ur and Mwa began to call it "our" island, but Ka told them that it was not "our" island, but "his" island, and he would decide what to do with it. He said that he would give his brothers none of the land unless they told him their secrets of fishing. Since both Ur and Mwa wanted land very badly, they agreed to part with their secrets. Ka then learned to fish as well as his brothers.

Since it was Ka who pulled up the islets, he had the right to decide what should be done with them. To Ur, because he was older and a good fisherman, he gave the largest islet with the best fishing area. Ka kept for himself the second largest islet because it had good land for farming and gardening. The other islet was given to Mwa because it also had a good fishing area. The three brothers named the islets after themselves, and these islets have these names to this day. The oldest brother, Ur, called his Urak; the youngest brother, Ka, named his Kahlap, and the smallest islet was named by Mwa, Mwandohn.

The mother of the three brothers was very much loved by them, but time passed, and she eventually died. After she was buried, a coconut tree grew up from her grave. Its first fruit was a dry, immature nut which had three corners, and so the boys named the corners of the nut after themselves in the order of their ages: Ur, Mwa, Ka. This was their valuable heritage from their mother. The tree produced many, many more nuts and these were planted on the three islets of Mwoakilloa. Because of the brothers, the Mwoakillese word for a young coconut is *urmwaka*.

There is evidence on Mwoakilloa today that this story is true. Coconut trees, the mother's gift from her grave, abound on all three islets. The largest taro patch is found today on Kahlap because Ka was the best farmer and the best fishing areas are found off Urak and Mwandohn because of the fishing skills of Ur and Mwa. Also, one can see today the line used by Ka to raise the islets in the form of a reef dividing the lagoon into two parts.

*Urmwaka of Mwoakilloa*

## THE DISCOVERY AND POPULATING OF PINGELAP

What is now known as the atoll of Pingelap was originally a sandbar discovered by two navigator brothers from Yap, Mwoimok and Palialap. After they found the sandbar, Palialap prepared to travel eastward toward what is now Kosrae, but Mwoimok set out to see if the sandbar extended beyond the horizon. Mwoimok traveled all morning and then he came upon two women, Lepond and Lipasapasan, who were carrying large baskets of fish and breadfruit. The women offered Mwoimok a bundle of preserved breadfruit. It was too large for his canoe, so the women tore it apart and gave half to Mwoimok, and then they disappeared.

Mwoimok returned to where he had left Palialap and told him of the barren reef that did not reach the horizon. But the area of the sandbar was very large and Palialap named it "Pingelap."

Later, Inohpas, the son of Palialap, arrived at Pingelap. He brought news of the three sons of Mwoimok named Riromau, Rikepik en Eir, and Pikepik en Epeng who had left Yap in search of him. So Mwoimok set out from Pingelap to find his three sons. He arrived back in Yap and after awhile married a woman named Damari. After the birth of their daughter, Nieri, they returned to settle on Pingelap. There, Nieri grew up and gave birth to three daughters and a son. From the daughters were born all of the people of Pingelap. The son, Iengir sang Eir, was selected as the first traditional leader of Pingelap.

Iengir-sang-Eir married a woman named Langedi who gave birth to a son, Kaupene. The name Kaupene means build together, and he became the second traditional leader, or Nahnmwarki, of the island. It is said on Pingelap that two poles cannot each stand alone, but leaning against one another they can support a heavy weight. Kaupene's name is symbolic of a society building together and the strength of a community working together. Kaupene also made the huge taro patch on Pingelap that is so necessary to the island and has continued to be in use generation after generation.

## HOW TOUHOU AT KAPINGAMARANGI WAS BUILT

Most of the people on the tiny Polynesian atoll of Kapingamarangi live on a small islet called Touhou. This islet is different from others on the atoll, and there is little doubt that it was made by man rather than nature. A story is told in Kapingamarangi about how this came about.

Long ago, during the time when idols and images were worshipped, it was decided by the people to build an island on the coral reef. It was planned that all of the people should work during the daylight hours, but never during the night. Then the people came together to pray and ask their gods for help.

On the first day they gathered large chunks of coral and put them together in piles. When the sun began to set, all of the workers returned to their homes to rest from the day's labor. The following morning when they returned to work, they were startled to find that the pile of rocks was very much larger than when they had left it the previous evening. They knew that something supernatural must be happening because all of the men had been at their homes sleeping during the night. They discussed this, and decided that it must be the work of their gods that was assisting them.

Day after day the people continued to work at building their island, and night after night the gods helped them. Finally, the islet was completed. It was high above the sea and was the most beautiful islet of the whole atoll.

The people planted many different food crops and built a very large hut in which they could worship their gods. After all of the planting and building were completed, they looked at their lovely new home and named it Touhou. (In the language of Kapingamarangi, *tou* means island and *hou* means new.)

An anchor was needed to keep Touhou from drifting away, and so a very large stone was brought by the gods from a distant island for this purpose. It was a volcanic stone, and the people placed it on the windward side closest to the breaking surf.

When all was completed, the people feasted, danced, and shouted for joy. They knew that so long as the stone anchor remained in its place, the island of Touhou would not drift away.

# *Kosrae Island*

## HOW KOSRAE VILLAGES WERE FIRST POPULATED AND NAMED

Kosrae is one of the largest islands in Micronesia. Although people can be found throughout the island today, there are still only four main villages, as there were in the past. A story is often told on Kosrae about how these four villages were first settled and how they were named.

It all began long ago with a mother, her three sons and her daughter, who stayed on a small portion of the island. As time passed, the mother grew to be very old and could no longer care for her children, so she called them together and told the children that it was time for her to let them go off on their own and find homes on the island.

The oldest son wandered westward until he came to a place he wanted for his home on the western part of Kosrae. He named this place Tafunsak. The name comes from two Kosraean words: *tafu*, meaning half, and *sak*, which means woods or trees. He named his home Tafunsak because when he arrived there he found the place to be half covered with woods. Today, Tafunsak is the largest village on Kosrae because it was first settled by the oldest son.

The lovely daughter of the old woman settled the second village on Kosrae, and she called her home Malem, meaning moon. She chose this name because it was night time when she arrived there and the moon was shining very brightly. Malem looked so very beautiful under the moonlight. Because the daughter settled there long ago, young girls from this village are the most beautiful on the island even today.

The next oldest son wandered a great distance from his mother until he came to the far side of the island. He could go no further, so he decided to settle there. He wanted a name for his home, but he could not think of an appropriate one. Then he remembered that when he wandered there he had come to the back to find his home, so he named it Utwe, meaning from the rear.

*Kosrae (circa 1830)*

The youngest son did not want to leave his mother and wander off to find a new home as his sister and brothers had done. Rather than leave his mother alone, he stayed with her until she died. When he was alone, he decided to name his home. As he looked around the whole area, he saw that it was completely surrounded by water. He decided to name it Lelu, meaning the inside of the lake.

The four villages of Kosrae still have their special qualities that can be traced back to the people who named them. Tafunsak is the largest because of the importance of an oldest son. From Malem come the most beautiful girls because it was settled by the lovely daughter of the old woman. Utwe is the village farthest south because the second son traveled the greatest distance to get there. And Lelu is very special. Even today it is the capital village of the island because it was the home of the mother and her last born son.

# *Marshall Islands*

## WHY KWAJALEIN HAS SEPARATE ISLETS

Kwajalein Atoll covers a vast area and is the largest atoll in the world. The islets are spread apart and a person could not possibly see the other islets from any one place. Also, today many of the islets are unpopulated, but in the past they all had people on them.

Long ago, when all the islets were very close together, a very beautiful woman appeared on Kwajalein. She came from nowhere. She was so beautiful that all of the landowners desired her. The landowners were called *alab* in Marshallese, and they were very greedy and jealous men. Since the islets were so close, a person could easily go from one to the other, and so no single *alab* could completely possess the beautiful woman.

The people did not know the name of the lovely woman so they called her Lien, which means "that lady" in Marshallese. Soon Lien disappeared, leaving all of the alab desiring her.

The landowners decided to move their islets away from each other so that when Lien reappeared, they would not have to compete for her. They wanted to move so far, in fact, that they could not even see each other. So the *alab* of Ebaten, the largest islet of Kwajalein, said, "Lien and my island, move to the west." And so the island moved westward. Then the *alab* of Roi Namur said, "Lien and Roi Namur, move north," and the island moved northward as soon as the words disappeared into the air. Then the owner of Kwajalein said, "Lien and my island, move to the south," and Kwajalein moved southward. All of the other *alab* also told their islands to move and so today they are so scattered that they are out of sight of each other.

Today, if a bird flew completely around the coral reef of Kwajalein atoll, it would see the results of the *alab* greed and jealousy. Ebaten is far from the rest of the islets and is even close to Lae Atoll. Roi Namur is located far away toward Likiep Atoll, and Kwajalein islet cannot be seen from either Ebaten or Roi Namur. It is located just near to Namu Atoll.

# II.
# The Origins of
# Reefs, Waters and Landmarks

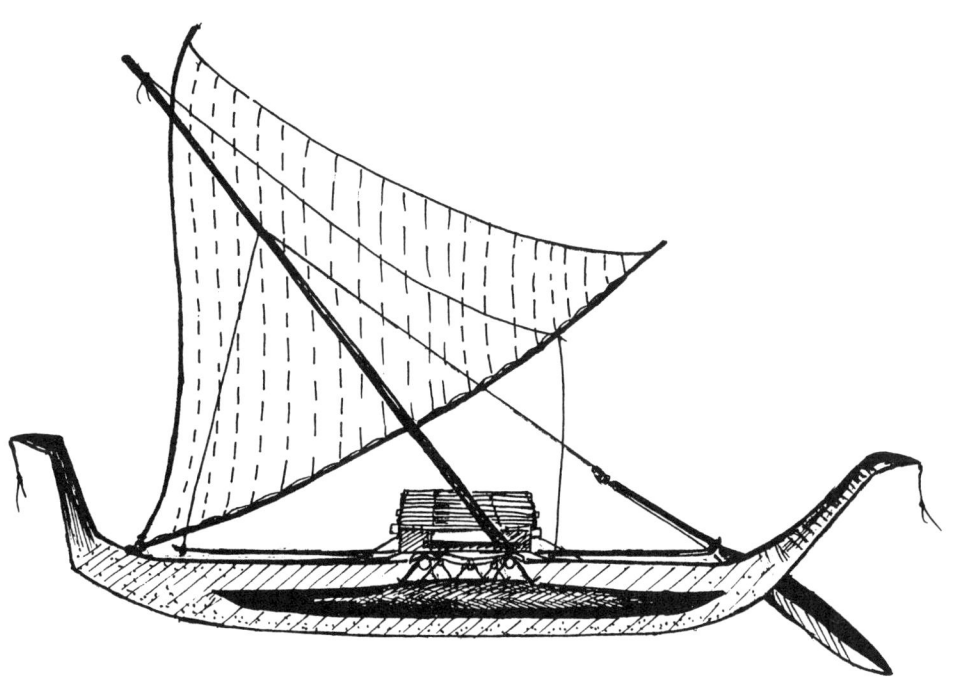

*Yapese Sailing Canoe*

*Palau Story Board*

# *Palau Islands*

## HOW A POOL LOST ITS SPELL AT NGERDMAU

Some older people desire to recapture their youth and become young again, while some young people seem anxious to grow up quickly. A story is told in a village of Ngerdmau municipality of Palau about how an old lady became young, and then found that she wanted to be old again.

There is a pool of water that can be seen today, and it is known in the area as the pool of returning youth. There is also a rock above the pool with the imprint of a child's foot stamped into it. According to legend, when an old person leaped into the pool, then youth would be immediately restored.

Many years ago an old woman was walking by this particular pool with her young daughter. It was a hot day and the two had traveled far, and so they stopped by the pool to rest. The old woman did not know the magic powers of the pool and so she decided to cool herself by leaping into the water. She told her daughter to wait on a nearby rock, and she jumped into the cooling pool.

The old woman dived deeply under the water, and when she resurfaced she was amazed to find herself turned into a young lady. She was so thrilled that she called her daughter to come and see her. But instead of running to her mother the young girl began to shout and cry and stamp her feet on the rock where she was standing. The child cried that the young lady was not her mother and refused to go near her.

The mother was in despair. She had regained her youth but lost her precious child. She was so upset that she again jumped into the pool and submerged. When she came back to the surface she was an old woman again and her child happily recognized her.

The old woman and the child were reunited, but in diving twice into the water, the woman had broken the magical power of the pool of returning youth.

Yet, to this day the pool is still called *Ngerchokl*, where youth is returned. Also, the rock where the young girl stamped her feet when her mother changed appearance still bears the imprint of the child's foot.

## WHY STONE FIGURES APPEAR AT NGERMID

There is a hamlet called Ngermid on Koror in the Palau Islands where long ago lived a widow and her young daughter.

In this small village, as in most villages in Palau, there was a large community meeting house called a *bai*. It was the custom each evening for people in the village to come to the *bai* for rest or recreation, or simply to exchange gossip. This *bai* was known to be inhabited by particular spirits who did not like the odor of fish. Because of this, it was a strict custom, always observed by everyone, to wash before entering the *bai*.

One day the widow and her daughter went to the shore to fish and to collect clams. They were so successful that they fished and collected clams throughout the afternoon until the approach of dusk. When they returned to Ngermid it was already dark and the village was deserted because everyone had gone to the *bai*. So they hurried home, left their fish, and rushed to the *bai* without pausing to wash themselves.

When they arrived at the meeting house and started to enter, everyone was shocked by the smell of fish on their bodies, and the people told the widow and her daughter to leave immediately and to wash before coming into the *bai* or something dreadful could happen to them. And just at that very moment the widow and her young daughter were turned to black stone. All of the people were startled and amazed and they returned to their homes thinking about the strange occurrence.

The next morning all of the people returned to the *bai*. And there stood the big rock figure of the widow holding her child in her arms.

Even today, any visitor to the meeting house in Ngermid can see the black figure of the old woman and her child who were turned to stone for ignoring a local custom.

## *Yap Islands*

### THE FIRST STONE MONEY OF YAP

Stone money on Yap is unique and heavy, both physically and culturally. It varies, like any other money, in both value and importance. The first money brought to the islands is considered to be the most valuable because of the distance between the rock quarries and Yap, and the age of the money.

History records Yapese as people of the sea. Long before foreign intrusion, Yapese navigators were sailing far and wide in what is now the Caroline Islands. Like other societies, the people of Yap considered money to be important, and the stone money was originally hewed in the islands of Yap.

There lived a man whose name is remembered as Fathaan on Rull Island in Yap. He realized that if money made in Yap continued to be produced, then it would lose its value because everyone would have as many pieces as he wanted. So Fathaan decided to sail to another island in search of a different kind of money. He then built his canoe and selected his crew for the journey.

Like other Micronesians of that time, he knew navigation. He used stars, the wind, the currents, floating vegetation, and birds as indicators as well as other natural forces to direct him.

After some time sailing, Fathaan reached the island of Palau. He and his crew went to a rocky area and worked at shaping this different stone into 150 discs, and no more. Then he brought his precious cargo back to Yap. To this day, these pieces are the most valuable of Yapese money and are called *Ngochol,* which means name. Any stone money brought after the first 150 pieces is not considered to be as valuable as the pieces of *Nigochol.* They are easily identified by Yapese who know stone money and cannot be counterfeited. Pieces of *Ngochol* are rougher than subsequent money because the first tools used were much more primitive than those used later.

*Yap Stone Money*

# Yap Outliers

## THE RED CORAL OF EAURIPIK

There is a special kind of coral of extreme beauty on Eauripik Atoll in Yap State. It has a special red color that can only be found on this particular island. It is of such great value that people will not sell it and only the natives of Eauripik can possess it.

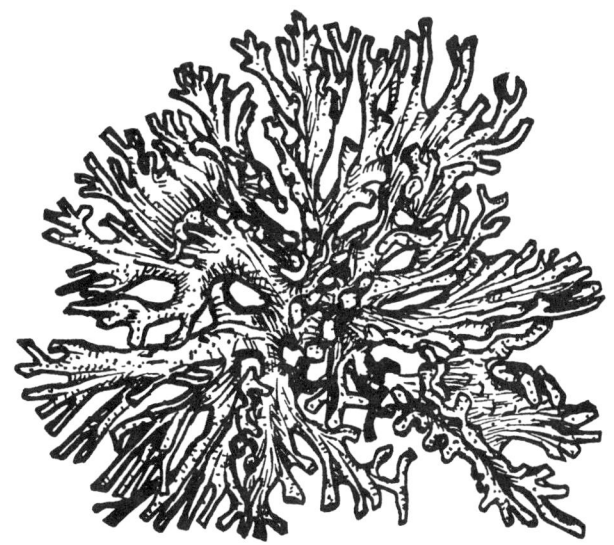

A beautiful girl named Has lived on the island. Her mother was from Ifalik and her father came from Eauripik. At that time, her mother happened to be away in Ifalik. One night Has had a frightening dream that her mother was very ill and almost dead. In the morning she told her father about the dream, but he paid little attention to her. The following night the girl again had the same terrible dream. When she again told her father about it he impatiently told her to stop talking about her mother. He said that if she kept talking about the dream and her mother, she would certainly get sick herself.

Every night the dream continued to repeat itself and Has' skin began to turn pale. Her father knew that if his daughter did not see her mother, Has would die, and so he decided to sail with her to Ifalik. He asked all of his relatives to prepare food for the voyage and he selected some men to accompany them as a crew. The party then set sail from Eauripik. After some time they arrived in Ifalik. There, Has completely recovered from her illness after being with her mother.

On Ifalik there lived a handsome young man named Tarau who had a lei of the most beautiful red coral. The girl admired the coral lei so much that she asked her relatives to kill Tarau and bring the lei to her. But Tarau learned of the plot on his life and so he sailed to Eauripik. Her father and Has immediately followed him. When Tarau saw their canoe returning he ran out to hide on the reef, but Has saw him and chased after him as fast as she could run. She ran after Tarau all over the reef until she finally caught up with him. Tarau, exhausted, then gave his beautiful red coral lei to Has and they walked back to the island together. As they were returning to Eauripik, Has decided to spread the coral on the reef so that everyone on the island could share it. When Has and Tarau got back to the island, she told all of the people about the beautiful red coral she had strewn across the reef. The coral grew, and today is shared by all of the people. It is theirs to keep, and cannot be taken away by any stranger without permission of the people on Eauripik.

## THE ROCK OF KHLOP ON SATAWAL

Some years ago two brothers lived together on Satawal. The older brother was called Katholab, meaning cruel, and his younger brother was Khlop, meaning kind. One day they decided to journey off together in seach of wives so that they could start their own families.

Katholab and Khlop walked together until the road separated. Each then took a different path. Khlop, after some time, came to a house where he saw something moving beneath a mat. He lifted the mat and found a girl with leprosy lying under it. She asked Khlop to please leave before he became infected with her disease. But Khlop felt great pity for the girl and instead of leaving, he asked her to marry him so that he could care for her. The girl, Lesor, meaning sunrise, was very impressed with Khlop's kindness. She asked him to return to his home and said that in time she would come to him.

Lesor's mother happened to be a goddess who had once made love to a mortal man. From this relationship, Lesor had been born. The infant had been so beautiful that her mother gave her the horrible disease to protect her by keeping others away. Lesor went to find her mother and told her of the kind man who had offered to care for her. She asked her mother to cure her of her horrible sickness. Her mother agreed to help, and led Lesor to a pond and told her to bathe. When she emerged from the pond, her leprosy had disappeared and she was startingly beautiful.

While waiting at his home, Khlop one day heard a knock at his door. He opened it to find the lovely Lesor before him. At first he did not recognize her, but when she kissed him he knew it was the girl he had found under the mat. He was so very happy to take the beautiful Lesor for his wife. Time passed and she bore him two sons and they all lived together in contentment.

Eventually, Katholab returned. He had been with many beautiful girls, but had seen none as lovely as Lesor. He became extremely jealous of his brother and tried to separate the couple by every possible means. But the love of Lesor and Khlop remained firm. Katholab became desperate and decided to do away with his brother, so one morning he asked Khlop to go fishing with him. When they were far from shore, Katholab hit Khlop a mighty blow in the head with a paddle and threw him overboard to drown. He then sailed alone back to Satawan.

Khlop's sons were waiting on the beach for their father's return, and Lesor was cooking food for the two brothers. When Katholab returned alone and said that Khlop had drowned, Lesor and her sons grieved and mourned terribly. Katholab lied that Khlop was eaten by a large fish when he dived under the canoe to free the anchor.

Time passed and the relationship between Lesor and Katholab grew closer. Finally, Lesor agreed to become the wife of Katholab since he was helping her so much by raising her sons. But when she told her children of her plans, they completely disapproved and said that they would leave home if she married their uncle.

The two sons of Khlop then left on a long journey to the place where the dead reside. There they found an old lady to whom they told their story, and she agreed to help them. She said some magic words and called forth all of those who died at sea from natural mishaps. Khlop was not among them. Then she said other magic words and called all of those who had been murdered at sea, and Khlop appeared in the ocean carrying a paddle. The old lady told the boys that their father had been killed by Katholab with the very paddle that he carried. She then gave the boys a fish net and told them she would call their father from the dead again. If they were able to catch him on the first attempt, then he would go with them back to life. If they failed, however, they would never see him again.

The boys were fortunate and caught their father in the net. They then placed him in special water that returned life to him, and they began sailing back to Satawal. As they approached, Lesor and Katholab were on the beach. They were to be married the next day. Katholab thought the distant approaching object was a turtle, a good omen before a marriage, and he hurried to the village to get assistance in catching it. But as the object came closer, Lesor recognized her husband and sons. She was suddenly elated, and she ran to the shoreline and hugged them when they beached their craft. Katholab shortly arrived with the villagers, and everyone was surprised to see Khlop alive and returned to Satawal. Katholab felt terrible shame, but Khlop offered forgiveness. He said that they were from the same womb and so he would take no revenge, but from that day onward they could never live together in the same house.

Katholab could not bear his own selfishness, and so he walked into the ocean. Then he told the people that he would turn himself into stone so that he could never bother Lesor and Khlop again. He then turned into a large rock that can be seen off of the beach of Satawal today. Khlop and Lesor lived on happily with their sons, and the stone has since then been known as "Faiul Khlop," or the Rock of Khlop.

*Men's House on Yap*

## WHY COCONUT TREES ARE PROMINENT ON WOLEAI

Today Woleai Atoll in the outer islands of Yap State is covered with coconut palms, but at one time there were none on the island. At that time, there lived a girl with her mother. They were very, very poor, and were rejected by other Woleaieans and forced to live alone at the far end of the atoll. The mother and daughter loved each other very much. The mother took good care of her daughter, protected her, and never let her play away from home.

One day when the mother left home to gather food, the girl became curious and ventured away from her house to the beach. There she saw a small eel lying helpless on the shore. The girl quickly wrapped the small creature in wet leaves and brought him to her home. She placed him in a pond where she could care for him, but she never told her mother about the eel. One evening her mother went to the same pond to bathe. When she saw the eel swimming, she was so shocked that she fainted. The daughter came to the pond a moment later and found her mother unconscious. She tried to revive her, but when she could not, she sat and cried because she felt so helpless. It was then that the eel spoke to the girl and told her to carry her mother home and let her rest, and to return to the pond the next morning. She did as she was told.

The following morning when the daughter returned, the eel was waiting. He told the girl that to repay her kindness for saving his life, he would help her mother to recover, but the girl had to promise to do exactly as she was told. She agreed. The eel then told the daughter to return that night with a sharp knife with which to cut off his head. The frightened girl, of course, was shocked and horrified, but she had given her word that she would do as instructed. Then the girl was told to take the head wrapped in leaves to the high ground in the middle of the islands where no one could see her and to bury it. She was told that in a few weeks an unfamiliar kind of tree would grow from the planted spot, and she must keep this secret from other people. When the tree began to bear fruit, she must pick the fruit, remove the husk, and find the hard shell in the center. On this shell she would see the eyes and mouth of the eel clearly visible. After opening the shell, she was told to feed the liquid to her mother, and she would awaken from her long sleep. The obedient girl did exactly as she was told, and soon her mother completely recovered.

This is how the first coconut palm was grown on Woleai. It also explains the secret of how the eyes and the mouth of the eel, who sacrificed his head, appear on every coconut, even today.

## HOW TARO WAS FIRST BROUGHT TO WOLEAI

At one time there was no taro on Woleai Atoll. Then a ghost caused it to appear. Later, most of the taro disappeared, but today it is abundant on the island.

There was living on Woleai a female ghost named Lorab who was always eating bananas, but she craved taro. She grew so tired of bananas that she decided to sail from Woleai in search of other food. She called a meeting of the people of Woleai and told them of her plan to find other food. The people helped her prepare for her journey. The next day they launched her large canoe and the ghost sailed away.

Lorab sailed north from Woleai until she found the islands of Fachaluk. The people there at first thought the canoe with its big sail was a large wave approaching them and they scattered to hide in the taro patches. When Lorab landed, she saw no one about and knew that the people must be hiding somewhere. She circled the island, but saw no people. Finally, she went into the taro patches and discovered the people hiding there. Lorab ordered all the people to fill her canoe with their taro, and if they failed to do so, she said she would eat all of the children on the island instead of the taro. The people were so afraid that they began harvesting the taro immediately, as fast as they could. By the next day, the entire area of the large canoe was filled with taro.

Lorab left Fachaluk knowing that all of the chiefs of Woleai would be happy with the taro. When she reached her island, she distributed the taro to all of the people to plant near their homes.

For many years, Woleai had very big taro patches, and they covered half of the island. On Fachaluk, however, there was only a small amount of taro left. But one day the Japanese came to Woleai. They took over the island and filled in the two biggest taro patches with soil so they could make aircraft runways. Now the airfield covers most of the old taro patches that Lorab helped to start, but Woleai still has more food growing than Fachaluk.

# *Truk Islands*

## THE TUNNEL OF PAATA

On the island of Paata, one of the Faichuk group in the Truk Islands, there lived a respected chief and his people. The chief resided on one side of Paata and the people lived on the other. It was difficult for the people to visit the chief because they had to walk around the island on the beach. Still, traditionally it was their responsibility to feed the chief and his family and to bring the best foods to him daily. There was only one way around the island to the chief's home.

One day a monster from the island of Polle near Paata came in search of food. When he arrived at Paata, he rested in the rocky mountains by the sea, just above the trail used by the people to visit their chief. Soon he smelled food that the people were carrying to their leader, and he jumped onto the path and robbed them. Time and time again the monster would take food from the people that was destined for their chief. He even threatened to eat the people if he did not get enough food.

Two turtles happened to be living on Paata at the time and saw the predicament of the people and decided to help. Together, they began to dig a tunnel through the middle of the island. They worked and worked until it was finished, and the people then had a new and safe route to use to visit their chief. It was not long before the monster became very weak from hunger, and he could not even move fast enough to catch people to eat. Finally he died of starvation and the people felt safe and rejoiced.

On the island today, one can still see the tunnel made by the two turtles. The opening is in the shape of a turtle's body from when they were digging the passage. Up to the present time, people of the island respect turtles and remember the help given that prevented them from being eaten by the monster of Polle.

## HOW AN OCTOPUS FORMED A MOUNTAIN ON MOEN

At one time, in the middle of Truk Lagoon, lived an extremely large octopus with enormous tentacles. He was acknowledged to be the chief of all undersea creatures. Whenever something was to be done, or a trip was to be taken, permission had to be granted by the octopus. He would also settle disputes that arose in the undersea community.

One day a shark asked the octopus for permission to swim to the surface and observe the activities of the land people. The octopus refused permission, saying that the shark could get into trouble on the unfamiliar surface of the lagoon. But the shark ignored the advice of the octopus and he swam to the surface despite the octopus' warning.

The shark saw people having all sorts of fun when he got to the surface, and he wanted to enjoy himself in the same way. When the shark saw an old man on the shore he asked if he could be included in the fun, and the old man said of course he could.

Several days passed and the shark did not return to the depths. So the octopus ordered all of the undersea creatures to search for him. Finally, a fish reported seeing the shark with land creatures, and this made the octopus furious because of the shark's disobedience. The octopus went to the surface himself to see the shark, but when he arrived there he found that the shark had been killed by the people. So the great octopus crawled up over the dry land and buried all of the people with his enormous body and long tentacles, but in doing so, the octopus also killed himself.

This event happened a very long time ago, and since then people have come from other places to populate Moen. But the large body of the octopus can be plainly seen today in the shape of a hill called Mt. Tonachau and also its large protruding tentacles as ridges toward the lagoon from which the octopus had come.

# *Truk Outliers*

## WHY SAND WAS EXCHANGED FOR SOIL ON MURILO

Ghosts are very well-known, especially to the children in Truk. One story told from the past is about how soil and sand was exchanged by ghosts from Murilo in the Hall Islands and Romolum in Truk Lagoon. These events occurred before the arrival of Christianity in the islands.

The ghosts of Murilo once gathered together for a meeting to decide where to find good soil for growing crops. Finally, after a lot of arguing, they decided to go to Romolum in Truk and steal the soil that they needed. That night they all prepared to leave.

For the journey they brought large sacks to carry the soil and tools for digging, but they brought no weapons. They arrived on Romolum at a village called Epin Fonu, filled their sacks, and flew back to Murilo. They emptied their sacks and returned again. The place where the soil was deposited was a small island called Enenias. At the time, the ghosts of Romolum were unaware of what was happening. But on the third trip by the ghosts from Murilo, those of Romolum were awake and they caught the thieving ghosts. The chief from Romolum assembled all of his people at Epin Fonu. They then beat the thieving ghosts and ordered them to return the stolen soil. The ghosts of

Murilo apologized, and asked to have a conference with the chief. The ghosts explained their reason for taking the soil and said that they were desperate for land in which they could grow food because all they had was sand on their island. The ghosts begged forgiveness from the chief and said that if he would forgive them, his people would receive something in return. The ghosts of Murilo then offered to bring sand to Romulum at the area from which they stole the soil. The chief agreed and the sand was brought and spread on Romolum all the way to the sea.

Today on Murilo, there is a small, rich area used for planting crops. And on Romolum, there is a small beach that is enjoyed by all of the people. It was brought there by the ghosts from Murilo.

## THE SWEET WATER OF EAST FAYU

There is water with a special sweetness found on East Fayu Island. This water was intended to be on Unanu, but it was spilled before it got there.

There once was a female ghost named Natuk living on the island of Unanu in Namonuito Atoll. She was a kind ghost and liked all of the people and the people were very kind to her. One day Natuk decided to voyage throughout the islands of Truk. She sailed from one island to another until at last she came to Moen. On Moen she went to the village of Peliesele. After her travels Natuk was very thirsty, so she rested to drink some water. She was amazed to find that the water of Peliesele had a delicious, sweet taste. Natuk thought how nice it would be to bring some of the water to the people of Unanu.

Natuk took a big gulp of the sweet water into her mouth without swallowing it, and this is the way that she would carry the water home. While returning to Unanu she was passing East Fayu and she heard singing, shouting, and laughter. She suddenly remembered that this was the time when all ghosts came to the island to perform their dances, and so she decided to delay her return so she could watch the festivities. She entered the large hut, the *ut*, and sat half-hidden in a corner. She stayed away from the other ghosts because she did not want to lose the water by being forced to talk to someone. Everyone in the *ut* laughed, and kept talking and shouting except for Natuk. She kept silent and only smiled when something humorous occurred.

Among the ghosts in the *ut* was Olofat, who was known for practical jokes and making fun of others. Looking around, he spied the smiling Natuk. He looked at her again and again and wondered why she spoke to no one, and he decided to find out the secret that she was hiding. Olofat left the *ut* and circled to the corner where Natuk was sitting. He then sneaked up on her from behind and surprised her by tickling her. Natuk could not prevent herself from giggling and laughing and so the water spurted out of her mouth. This made her very upset and angry and she criticized Olofat fiercely for his practical joke.

So the water was spilled onto East Fayu and never reached Unanu. It settled into the ground, where it remains to this day. If one digs a hole on the island, even on the beach close to the saltwater, one will find the sweet, fresh water spilled by Natuk when she was tickled by Olofat.

*Ut on East Fayu*

## HOW COCONUT CRABS CAME TO EAST FAYU

Natuk, the female ghost, is well-known in the Western Islands of Truk. It is thought that she was responsible for bringing the many coconut crabs to the island of East Fayu. The crabs are no longer there, but at one time they nearly covered the island.

Once Natuk traveled to meet a magician named Souwariras in Moen in Truk Lagoon hoping to get some food for her people. Upon her arrival, no one greeted or welcomed her, so she decided to steal the food that she needed. She went to the large meeting house where there was a lot of food and saw a coconut crab already eating and roaming around the food that had been placed there. She thought the crab was Souwariras, and went closer to grab some food. Then, Natuk suddenly started laughing and said, *Pwota ina me atengawom*, meaning "What an ugly chief!" The crab felt ashamed at Natuk's remarks and crawled away quickly to the shore, as scared coconut crabs do. There, the crab hid itself in Natuk's sailing canoe.

Natuk took all of the food that she wanted to her canoe and prepared to leave Moen. After sailing for some time, she sighted a small island and decided to head for it. When she was near the shore, though, she fell asleep and the crab escaped and jumped onto the island. It turned out to be East Fayu. When Natuk awoke, she had drifted away from the island, so she continued her journey homeward.

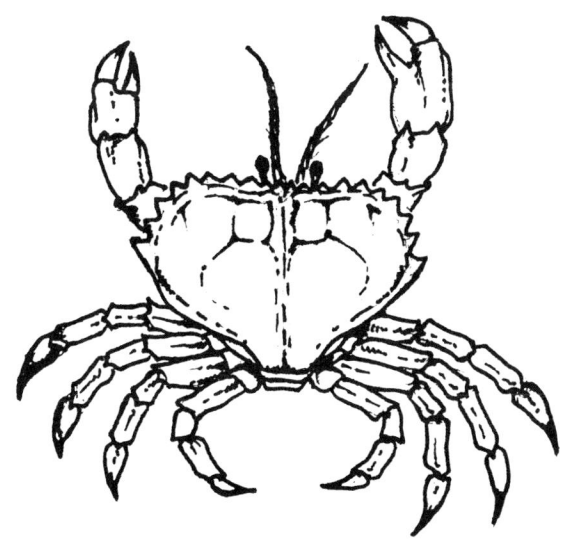

The coconut crab was pregnant and laid many eggs shortly after arriving at the new home. Soon, many small crabs were born. As navigators arrived on the island to hunt for turtles and turtle eggs, they always left the crabs alone because they were thought to represent ghosts that were on the island. For many years, fishermen would visit and do no harm to the crabs, but then the coconut crabs began to disappear. Fishermen began to collect them and no one really knows why. Perhaps the story of Natuk had been forgotten or disbelieved, or perhaps the fishermen were from Moen, but at any rate the coconut crabs originally brought by the ghost Natuk are now extinct on East Fayu.

## HOW NAMOLUK LOST ITS BRAVE WARRIORS

Long ago, during the time of wars between the islands, Namoluk was known far and wide as the most productive island. The men were strong and brave, and they were great warriors. No outsiders would dare attack Namoluk. If they tried, they would either be killed or chased away. In fact, the warriors of Namoluk made numerous successful raids and invasions on the other islands in the lower Mortlocks.

The small island of Moch on Satawan Atoll made an alliance with the warriors of Namoluk. Because Moch was so small and had little food, the people of Namoluk allowed their allies to get food from their island.

At first, the people of Moch were very happy and would come to Namoluk and then return with their canoes full of food. But soon they grew weary of the thirty-mile journey between the islands. They wanted to take over Namoluk but knew that they could not defeat their brave allies in battle. Their desire was so great to take over Namoluk that they decided to defeat its warrors by magic.

One day a canoe from Moch appeared close to the reef off of Namoluk. Recognizing that it came from Moch, the men did nothing to disturb it. When the canoe reached the mouth of the channel, it stopped. A certain magic was then applied that would make all of the men leave the island. When this was done, the canoe sailed farther offshore so it would not be affected by its magic spell.

The elders of Namoluk leisurely watched the canoe. But when they saw it leaving the island instead of entering the channel, they immediately knew something evil had taken place. They rushed for protection, but it was too late. The magic from Moch had already started to take effect.

Very soon all of the brave men of Namoluk lost their minds and went crazy. They became so fearful of their own island that they rushed to a small portion of the coral reef for protection. There they remained until every one of them perished.

When the news spread that Namoluk was left unprotected, people from other islands in the Mortlocks rushed to settle the island. As a result, the people of Namoluk today have many relatives throughout the Mortlocks. Also, the reef on which all of the brave warriors died is known even today as the Reef of the Men.

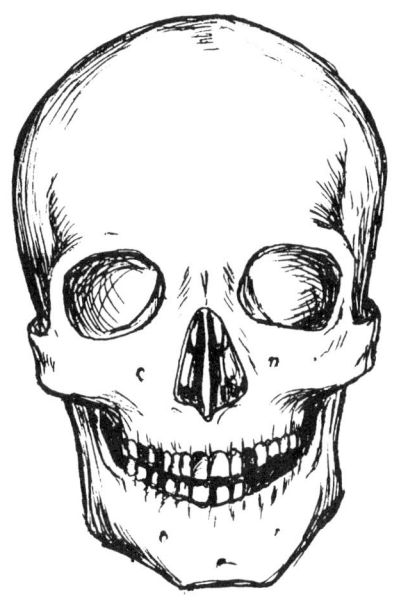

## HOW A SANDBAR WAS FORMED ON LOSAP

A particular sandbar near Losap had a characteristic of pounded breadfruit. The sand moves when one steps on it, but then returns to its original shape. This sandbar was formed because two greedy boys did not follow instructions from a ghost.

At one time there was a mysterious famine on Losap. This was particularly unusual because Losap has always been known for its abundant food. But when breadfruit, coconuts and taro ripened, they would suddenly disappear, and the large fish in the sea could not be caught.

Days and weeks passed. Many people became sick and some even died from starvation. The people were so weak that only a little fishing took place. One night two brothers and their sister went to the reef to try to catch a few small fish. They carried torches to light their way and went far from their home. But it rained, the torches were extinguished, and they were all plunged into darkness.

The two boys and the girl headed back toward shore when they suddenly saw a light gleaming from the middle of the taro patch. They went toward the light and began to enter the taro patch. At that moment they heard a strange voice warning them that women and men who smelled of fish must not enter the taro patch, so the boys bathed and their sister remained near their canoe.

The smell of cooking taro was tantalizing to the brothers. The boys entered the patch, and came upon a ghost-woman who was baking taro. She knew they were hungry so she gave each of them a portion of taro to eat. But the boys were not satisfied and whispered to each other about getting more food. The ghost-woman, however, heard everything the boys were saying.

Since the brothers were tired from the night's activities, everyone went to sleep. The next morning the boys told the ghost-lady that they must return home or their parents would worry. So the ghost-lady prepared a small portion of pounded breadfruit for them and wrapped it in a green leaf. She warned them, however, not to open the food until they reached home safely.

The boys left the ghost-lady and had hardly started their journey home when they opened the food, against the ghost-lady's warning, and they did not offer any to their hungry sister. All of a sudden the pounded breadfruit grew larger and larger and the boys had to throw it overboard to keep the canoe from sinking. The pounded breadfruit formed a sandbar that can be seen today. And when one walks on the sand, it immediately returns to its original shape, just like the pounded breadfruit given to the boys by a ghost-woman.

## THE LARGE PAPAYA OF NAMA

There is a place on a hill on one island of Truk State where papayas grow to an enormous size. On Nama Island, southwest of Truk Lagoon, they grow to be two feet in length and larger at a particular

location. Long ago, however, neither the papaya nor the hill could be found on Nama because the island was completely flat.

One day the chief of Nama called all of his people together to discuss a way to add a mountain to the island. The ghost of Nama heard about the discussion and offered to assist the chief in his effort. The ghost knew that there were many mountains in Truk Lagoon, so he flew off to take some soil from the highest one on Moen. When the Nama ghost had dug away a lot of soil, the ghosts of Moen saw him and chased him away. As he hurried away from the island, he dropped most of the soil and it formed islands along the way that are visible in Truk Lagoon today. When he finally reached Nama, the soil remaining was only the dirt that clung to his fingernails. He scraped this dirt out and it became a little hill on Nama instead of the mountain that had been hoped for.

And the hill on the small island of Nama is very evident to this day. It has soil more fertile than the rest of the island and it is rich in phosphate. In the stolen dirt, papayas have been planted over the years and they grow to be bigger than watermelons.

## WHY A BROTHER AND SISTER WERE TURNED TO STONE

Thunder and lightning are fearful experiences for children, and often they will shout when they occur because they are so frightened. However, the children of Nama, in the Upper Mortlock Islands, are not permitted to shout or to show fear when a thunderstorm occurs. They are reminded by their elders of what can happen if they shout when seeing lightning or hearing thunder, and are told a story about a boy and a girl in a thunderstorm.

On Nama lived a young brother and sister. They were inseparable, and loved each other very much. One day they decided to go fishing, even though the heavy rain indicated that a storm was approaching. They were warned about the danger, but they did not listen.

As they walked from their houses with their fishing poles, there was thunder and lightning in the distance. They went onto the reef and got hermit crabs in shells for bait, and then went out further on the reef to fish.

Suddenly there was lightning overhead, followed by a loud crack of thunder, and both children shouted loudly. Then the lightning flashed again and the brother and sister shouted even more loudly.

Then again and again the lightning and thunder occurred, and each time the children would shout in fear. Finally, a lightning bolt struck so close to them that the boy and girl were swept into the sea and were drowned. But instead of sinking or floating away, they were turned into coral images of a boy and girl with fishing poles in their hands.

If one goes to Nama, the coral figures of the boy and girl can easily be seen, half covered by the sea that swept them to their deaths. Also, the people of Nama tell their children not to shout during thunder and lightning or they too will be turned into coral like the unfortunate brother and sister who went fishing in a storm.

## WHY A REEF WAS FORMED AT SATAWAN

Satawan Atoll consists of numerous islets with a circular reef connecting them. Two of these islets belong to the clan of a small man named Olusa, and a portion of the reef is said to be the grave of a giant named Melow.

Melow was a gigantic man from Moch on Satawan Atoll, an islet facing Kuttu across the lagoon. Some say he was as tall as a breadfruit tree. One day Melow came to Kuttu and frightened all of the people and took their crops, meat, and other possessions. Word quickly spread of this fearful giant, and all of the people were afraid except for a small man named Olusa, who was working in a taro patch.

The traditional chiefs gathered to find a solution on how to handle the problem of Melow. They met and discussed what to do, but in the end they could find no answers.

One day the people of Kuttu were shouting for fear as they saw Melow approaching. Olusa, the small man, was again away working in the taro patch at that time. When he heard all of the commotion, he quickly hurried to find out exactly what was happening. He was told that the giant Melow had again come and robbed and frightened the good people of Kuttu.

Olusa decided to help his people. When everyone returned to their homes he began his journey to find the giant. He walked in front of the islets where the lagoon was most shallow. Soon the tide began to rise higher and higher until only Olusa's head was above water.

When Melow first saw Olusa, he thought he was seeing a coconut or a taro root floating on the water. Then suddenly Melow recognized Olusa, and as the little man walked toward him, Melow laughed loudly to think that little Olusa would challenge him to a fight.

Olusa attacked giant Melow, and the giant immediately picked him up and threw him into the lagoon. Olusa swam back to the shore and attacked Melow again. And again the giant threw the little man into the sea. Time and again Olusa attacked Melow, and time and again Olusa was thrown back into the lagoon. Finally, the giant grew so tired from throwing Olusa that he was only able to drop the little man at his feet. Olusa had exhausted Melow and the giant was powerless. Suddenly, Olusa grabbed a large oyster shell, struck the giant fiercely, and killed him.

Olusa then returned to Kuttu and told his people that he had killed the fearful Melow. The people were jubilant, and the chief was so pleased that he gave two islets on Satawan Atoll to the small hero. These islets, Pike and Meriong, the sea that touches them, and the coral reef beyond are owned by the clan of Olusa to the present day.

A number of men acccompanied Olusa back to see the body of the giant. Then they buried Melow in the sea beside the islet. Soon a reef was formed on top of the grave of Melow that extended into the lagoon, and this reef can be clearly seen today on Satawan Atoll.

## WHY A CHANNEL APPEARS AT ETTAL

Ettal in the Mortlock Islands of Truk had been protected from typhoons for many years by a magician named Kupil. The spell was lost when the magic medicine of Kupil was spilled by accident.

Whenever a typhoon was heading toward Ettal, Kupil would always walk around the island with his secret medicine. He would spread it around, and this would protect the people from being hit by a typhoon. In 1963, a severe storm called Emy headed toward Ettal. By then, Kupil was very old, and could hardly walk. But he roused himself and took his medicine and gathered his strength to walk. When he reached the end of Ettal, he stumbled and fell to the ground, and his medicine was scattered all around. People ran to help Kupil, but he had already died.

The people knew that from the time of Kupil's death, the place where he fell would change into a channel because of the spilled medicine if another typhoon struck. When the coming of the next storm was announced, all of the people hurried away from the area where the medicine had been spilled to find safer places.

In 1976, a typhoon named Pamela struck Ettal. Although it destroyed homes and uprooted trees, no one was seriously injured. As a result of the typhoon, however, the area on which the medicine was scattered really was changed into a channel as was predicted and is called *A Much*, which means "it is finished" in Mortlockese. The words are a remembrance of Kupil and his protective medicine that no longer protected the people from typhoons.

# *Pohnpei Island*

## THE GIANTS AND THE TRIDACNA SHELLS

There once lived a couple at a small place on Pohnpei. In the center of the area there was a fish pond, but giants lived near to it. The clan of the couple and the children could go anywhere, but the children were told to stay away from the pond of the giants. One day the children were disobedient and went to the pond of the giants where they caught a fish and then they hurried home. When the giants discovered that one of their fish was missing, they hid and waited to find out who would dare take fish from their pond. After some time, a group of children returned to the giants' pond and speared another fish. When the giants saw this, they ran after the children who hid under some very large tridacna shells. When the giants demanded that the children be given to them, the giants were told to reach in and get the children themselves. The giants then tried to grab the children and the tridacna shells clamped down on the giants and killed them. Instead of the giants making a meal of the children, the giants became a meal themselves. From that time onward, the land has belonged to the tradacna shells.

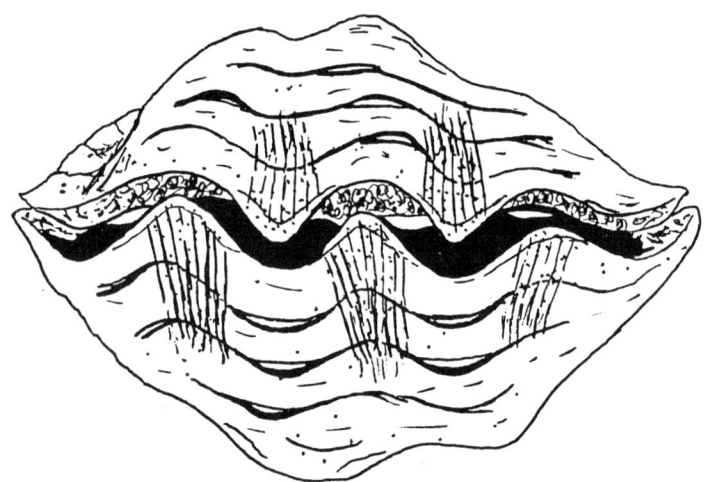

## HOW SOKEHS ROCKED WAS FORMED

A most prominent feature of Pohnpei Island is Sokehs Rock which reaches a height of 662 feet above the entrance to Kolonia Harbor on mountainous Sokehs Island. The rock is actually called *Peipalap* by Pohnpeians, and at one time neither the mountains or the rock existed.

When Sokehs Island was flat, a spring shot out from the ground and formed a very fast moving stream. One day a man wanted to cross the stream and he waded in. When he was in the center, the fast current grabbed him and carried him all the way to Katau, which some say is Kosrae. When he arrived there a man named Tsou Peipalap met him and asked where he had come from and how he got to Katau. The man told Tsou Peipalap about his island called Sokehs and the fast-moving stream that carried him to Katau. Tsou Peipalap had magical powers, and the two men returned to Pohnpei together. When they arrived at Sokehs, the stream was still surging from the ground with a tremendous speed. Tsou Peipalap took a large stone and hurled it into the opening of the spring and plugged the hole. He named the stone after himself, *Peipalap,* and the stone grew and continued to grow into the Sokehs Rock that we see today.

*Peipalap, Sokehs Rock at Pohnpei*

## NARUHPE'S POOL IN MADOLENIHMW

At Lohd, in Madolenihmw, there was a woman who had three daughters. The youngest was the most beautiful among all of the girls of Pohnpei. She had a particular pond in which she would bathe daily and the pond flowed into the sea. Whenever she would bathe, fragrant oil from her skin would float away into the ocean.

There lived at that time on Ant Atoll a man named Soulik en Ant who was very cruel. One day the oil from the skin of the lovely woman floated all the way to Ant and was found by Soulik en Ant. He was so excited by the oil that the decided to sail to Pohnpei and take its owner for his wife. He then assembled all of his men to accompany him to Madolenihmw.

Many canoes sailed from Ant to Pohnpei. When they arrived, Soulik en Ant sent a messenger to the old woman telling her that he was taking her youngest daughter for his wife. But the mother loved her young daughter dearly, so she sent her eldest daughter as a bride to deceive Soulik en Ant. But the man from Ant was not fooled, and he sent the eldest daughter back to the old lady. The mother then sent her next oldest daughter to be the wife of Soulik en Ant. But again he was not fooled and he sent the woman back to her mother and demanded the youngest daugher. The poor old lady could do nothing but obey the wishes of Soulik en Ant.

After the arrival of the lovely young girl, all of the canoes then sailed back toward Ant. On the way back, Soulik en Ant became more and more furious because he had been deceived by the old woman, so he threw the young girl into the sea. As she was sinking, her long hair became tangled in the outrigger of the canoe of a man named Kanikin Ant. Sharks immediately attacked her and her whole body was devoured except for her lovely face.

Kanikin Ant felt such love and pity for the girl that he pulled her head from the sea. When he returned to Ant he took the head to his house and wrapped it in taro leaves and hid it in a different house. A few days passed and Kanikin Ant went to the house again to see the lovely face of the dead girl. When he opened the door he was startled to see that the girl had come back to life and was sitting combing her long hair. He was so happy to see her that he took her for his wife.

The evil Soulik en Ant heard what had happened. He was so jealous that he planned a cruel deception. He would hold a feast and invite everyone so that Kanikin Ant could not fail to come. Then he would murder him and reclaim the young girl for his wife.

The feast took place and everyone attended, including Kaniken Ant and his bride. But the girl knew of Soulik Ant's evil plan and so she did not participate in any of the activities. All she did was put more and more coconut husks on the fire. When the smoke was very dark and thick, she and Kanikin Ant leaped into it and the smoke carried them together back to Lohd. There they happily stayed together for the rest of their lives.

This legend is also known to be true in Madolenihmw. The young girl's name was Naruhpe, and her bathing pool and the nearby taro patch can be seen clearly in Lohd to this day.

## *Pohnpei Outliers*

### HOW A RIVER WAS STOLEN FROM MWOAKILLOA

The Marshall Islands and Mwoakilloa Atoll in Pohnpei State have long been related. It is even known that people from the Marshalls settled on Mwoakilloa after a severe typhoon struck the island centuries ago. A mutual problem of both the Marshalls and Mwoakilloa is a continuous supply of water, and this came about because of the jealousy of three women over one man.

A gigantic man named Lodup lived on Mwoakilloa long ago, and many stories are told about his power. He was known to be quite strong, but was very, very lazy. Instead of working his land, Lodup always preferred to have others do the work for him.

One day Lodup left his home and sailed to the Marshall Islands in his large canoe. When he returned, he was accompanied by three beautiful Marshallese women whom he had married. Lodup was smart enough to not keep the women together because they would be very jealous of one another, so he put one on each of the three islets of Mwoakilloa: Kahlap, Mwandohn and Urak.

Each of the wives had magical powers and each loved Lodup and wanted to be the first in his affection. The favorite wife of Lodup, however, was the one he had sent to Kahlap, the largest of the three islets.

At that time, Kahlap had a special quality as well as its size. All kinds of vegetation would grow there because of its fertile soil and water supplied from the only stream on Mwoakilloa. The two wives on the other islets were extremely jealous because Lodup spent so much time with the woman on Kahlap. The wife who lived on Mwandon happened to be related to the royal family in the Marshalls, the *Iroij*, and was particularly upset. So one night she crossed the reef to Kahlap and sang her magic songs beside the river. As she finished her chanting and singing, the river disappeared and flew away to Sapwalap in Madolenihmw on Pohnpei.

When Lodup's wife on Kahlap went to her river, she found that it was gone. She then hurried to Urak, but found no one on the islet. Then she went to Mwandohn, but found it to be deserted too, and she suspected that the other two wives had returned to the Marshall Islands. She went to the house of the wife on Mwandohn and there she performed her strongest magic. This caused all of the rivers in the Marshalls to either dry up or disappear to Pohnpei.

All of the rivers in the Marshall Islands are now gone, and also the one on Mwoakilloa, because of the jealous wives. The river stolen from Mwoakilloa is known on Pohnpei as Lehn Mokil, the former name of Mwoakilloa.

## THE GHOST ROCK OF MWOAKILLOA LAGOON

A large rock sits in the lagoon of Mwoakilloa. It is known as the Ghost Rock, and older people on the island say that the rock was once a woman.

The woman of whom the older people speak was the wife of the chief and she died giving birth. The child also died and the spirit of the woman was so enraged that she chased everyone, including the chief, away from the island where the mother and child had died. After escaping hurriedly, the chief remembered that he had left some of his belongings and much of his treasure on the island with the mad spirit. The chief asked for volunteers to return to the place and retrieve his things, but even the bravest men were afraid to go. Finally, a young man came forward out of the group and said he would try to help the chief. So happy and relieved was the chief that he promised the young man that he would be the next chief if he was successful.

The swiftest canoe on the island was prepared for the young man, and he placed a large black rock in the center of the craft. When he sailed to the island, he found the ghost sleeping. He very silently gathered the chief's belongings and took them to his canoe. When he was about to leave, he accidentally stepped on a dried coconut frond and the crackling noise awakened the ghost. He quickly leaped into his canoe and began paddling furiously, but the ghost also paddled fast in her boat. As rapidly as he could paddle, the ghost still was gaining on him and nearly reached his canoe. Suddenly the young man threw the heavy rock he had brought with him overboard. When the ghost heard it splash, she thought it was the chief's treasure, and she dove underwater after it as the young man hurried back to the safety of his island.

The ghost went all the way to the bottom of the lagoon, only to find a black rock instead of a treasure. She was so upset at being tricked and not finding any treasure that she died on the spot and was turned into the black rock that one sees in the lagoon as the Ghost Rock even to this day.

## THE STINGRAY'S CREVICE ON MWOAKILLOA

On Mwoakilloa, childbirth used to be a mysterious process to the people. Since modern methods of delivering babies were unknown during this time, pregnant women knew no happiness and were constantly in fear of childbirth. The procedure in having a baby was fearful. When a woman was nearly ready to deliver, she would be taken to Urak, a large islet of the atoll, and put in the charge of an old man. This was the only person on the island, and his duty was to operate on women by cutting their wombs open just before delivery and pulling out their babies.

It happened that the chief's daughter got pregnant. This made the chief very fearful for her, and he was so sad that he could not even eat. The girl protested, but the chief had to send her away because it was the custom. When it was nearly time for her to deliver, he ordered some men to take his daughter to Urak for the operation. When they arrived on the islet, the girl managed to escape and hide in the center of Urak.

One night while she was sleeping, a stingray appeared near her just before she was ready to have her labor pains. The stingray told her not to be afraid and that he would help deliver her baby. Soon the baby was born without being torn from the girl's womb. This made her so happy that she promised to give away her baby to the stingray. She told the stingray to return in four days for the infant. In three days, people from her clan found the girl and everyone was very happy and relieved to see the mother and child alive and well. The new mother was so excited that she forgot her promise to the stingray and left for her home with the child.

When the stingray returned to the place where he was to meet the mother and child four days later, he found they had disappeared. This made the stingray so furious that he scraped all of the sand, coral, trees, and anything else in his way into the lagoon of Mwoakilloa. Today one can see on Urak a large indent in the island that was caused by the angry stingray who was unable to take a new-born baby.

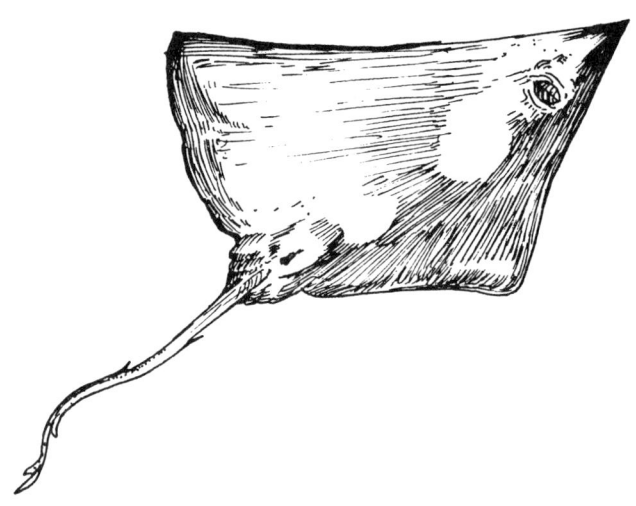

## WHY THE ISLETS OF PINGELAP ARE SEPARATED

A stretch of lagoon sits between the islets of Deke and Sukoru on Pingelap Atoll at present. At one time, however, these islets were a single piece of land. They became separated when a god from the Marshall Islands visited the atoll and caused the lagoon to form.

On the western side of Jaluit Atoll in the Marshalls, at an area sticking out from the rest of the land, sits an islet named Pingelap. It has this name because it is placed at the exact spot where the god took sand from Pingelap in Pohnpei State and deposited it at Jaluit.

Long ago the people of Pingelap worshipped a god named Isopaw. He was a lazy god and his greatest pleasure was sleeping away the days. He would only awaken briefly at night. On a day while Isopaw was sleeping, another god from Jaluit appeared on Deke. He was careful not to awaken Isopaw, and he took a gigantic handful of sand from the area causing a trench to form that became a lagoon between Deke and Sukoru. The people watched this unusual happening, and then they immediately awakened Isopaw and told him the news. Isopaw asked in what direction the other god had gone, and was told that it was directly to the east. Isopaw then hurried after the strange god.

By the time that Isopaw caught up with the other god, they had traveled all the way to Jaluit. When the Marshallese god saw Isopaw, he dropped all of the sand that he was carrying and hurried away. The sand was spread over such a large area of the reef that Isopaw could not hope to pick it all up, so he left it all on Jaluit and returned to Pingelap.

From that time onward, a lagoon has separated Deke from Sukoru. This is at the exact place where the Marshallese god scooped up the sand while Isopaw slept. Also, there is an islet on Jaluit that is named after this incident, and this is where the god dropped the sand when being chased by Isopaw.

# *Kosrae Island*

## THE STONE FOOTPRINTS AT WALUNG

At the far end of Tafunsak, the largest village on Kosrae, there is a place called Walung. Here sits a large rock known to all of the people in the area because of a strange imprint of two sets of footprints in the stone. One set is of a man and the other is of a young woman.

Long ago there lived a king and a queen in Lelu, the capital village of Kosrae. The queen was of such beauty that the king continually spoiled her by providing her with anything she desired. In Lelu also at this time lived a young girl, who was very beautiful, named Kumal. Because of her loveliness, the king selected Kumal from all of the women of Lelu to serve as the first-maid to the queen. This, of course, was a great honor indeed for Kumal. The queen was quite happy with the young Kumal, and treated and trusted her like a daughter.

There happened to be a very handsome young man named Fung living with his parents at the far end of Tafunsak quite distant from Lelu. His poor parents were getting quite old and they wanted very much for their son to marry before they died.

The queen found out about this extremely handsome young man. Since she had always had anything she desired, she decided to capture this man and keep him for herself. So she gathered all of her maids and servants together to make a plan to capture him. It was decided that the queen would lead them in a long line from Lelu to Walung. The lovely Kumal would walk second behind the queen.

As the line of maids and servants marched toward Tafunsak, it became spread out. No one knew that the handsome Fung was hiding behind a rock at Walung watching the line approach. After seeing the queen in the lead, he was dazzled by the beauty of Kumal who was not far behind. As the lovely young girl passed near the rock, he grabbed her and remained hidden from sight until all the others had passed by. The couple immediately fell in love with each other as the line of maids and servants disappeared into the distance. They sat with their feet on the rock and talked of their love and future together.

When the queen and her entourage reached the parents' home, she found only the old people present and became very angry. She asked the whereabouts of the son, but the parents would only say that he was gone and would not return for some time. The queen did not believe this and became furious because she could not have what she desired. She ordered her servants to burn the house to the ground with the old people inside.

The house burned, and the wind carried the ashes to the rock where the young people were happily resting. Both Kumal and her lover, Fung, realized what had happened, and with hands held tightly together, they ran toward the burning house. The queen feared that the young couple might leap into the flames to save the parents or to die with them, so she ordered her servants to circle the flaming house to prevent this. Before the order could be obeyed Kumal and Fung rushed into the inferno to die with the parents. The queen, unable to accept the humiliation of her own failure, also ended her life.

And so the Rock of Walung remains at the far end of Tafunsak to this day, with the footprints of the two lovers clearly visible where they sat. It is a reminder of a tragic death of the couple, a cruel queen, but also of the sacrifice of children for their parents.

## THE SLEEPING WOMAN AND THE WHALE

The island of Kosrae has two prominent physical features

that are very mysterious to visitors arriving on the island. One is the shape of the islet of Lelu, on the fringe reef off of the island. On any map, it distinctly resembles the carcass of a monstrous whale. The other is the peaks of the mountains above Lelu. They look exactly like a sleeping woman, perpetually resting above the harbor.

Many years ago, the prominent islet of Lelu did not exist. At that time, a great disaster was taking place on Kosrae in the form of a giant who was satisfying his appetite by eating the poor people of the island. To save their lives, there was a mass migration from Kosrae, and all of the people sailed away in canoes except for one lone young woman.

By herself, this girl fled high into the mountains for protection. It was not long, however, before she became very hungry and left her hideaway in search of food. The tide was low when she reached the fringing reef at the shoreline. There, she was startled to see a monster whale stuck on the coral.

The young woman made a very long rope and tied it to the whale so that it could not escape, and then she took one end of the rope and went into the mountains to rest. When the tide began to rise, the whale was forced to remain on the reef and could not swim away into the ocean.

Years passed, and both the girl and the whale died at the same time. Gradually, sand and soil formed on the carcass of the whale, and grass and shrubs grew around the young woman. Trees and other vegetation grew, and birds brought life to the sleeping girl and the dead whale. In the meantime, the giant had disappeared.

Many years later, the people who had fled returned to Kosrae. They were amazed to see a new fertile island just beyond the mainland. They landed on Lelu, and liked it so much that they made it the capital of all of Kosrae. But their joy was mixed with sadness as they saw the young woman asleep forever on the mountain.

These landmarks remain to this day—Lelu in the shape of a whale in the harbor, and the form of a girl at rest on top of the mountain above.

## WHY SHARKS SMELL OF URINE

There is a channel and harbor on the north of Kosrae called Okat. This place is quite famous on the island because of a group of strong, brave men who cooperated to defeat a monster.

This monster was dwelling in a section near a river. There were no roads on Kosrae in the old days, and so people used Okat Channel as their main highway. The only vehicles for transportation were outrigger canoes. When the people passed the dwelling place of the monster, he would command that half of the people in the canoes remain with him and the other half could go on. This meant that those who stayed with the monster would be eaten by him. It was usual that those who were old or physically weak were the unlucky ones. If the people refused the monster's demands he would chase after them and kill them all.

The monster brought shame and despair among the people of Kosrae. The population of the island decreased while the monster's belly grew larger and larger. The king at that time feared that all of the people would eventually be eaten so he organized a group of his bravest men to go and eliminate the monster forever. They made careful plans on how this might be accomplished.

The group of brave warriors, which consisted of twelve men, embarked on their fearful task. When they rowed to the home of the monster, he called out asking how many people were in the canoe. The warriors responded that there were twelve men. The monster said that six must stay and that the rest were free to go, but none of the warriors stayed to be eaten, and so the monster left his cave to pursue them.

The monster chased after the warriors and they fought a terrible battle as they reached the lagoon at Okat Harbor. At last the monster was killed by the brave warriors. His dead body was then thrown into the lagoon. The corpse did not float for long, as fish quickly gathered to eat it. Also, many sharks came and drank the monster's urine, and this is the reason for a urine smell all over sharks' bodies.

## REVENGE ON A CRUEL KING

Most events in stories on Kosrae took place before the arrival of the American missionaries in the middle of the 1800s. At the time, the island was ruled by chiefs or kings, some of them kind, but many tyrannical. The following tale is about a king who was very cruel and how he and a family were destroyed by the king's actions.

There was a woman named Sepe who had two loving sons, Kilafwa and Kun. They lived in the village of Tafunsak in the north of Kosrae. The oldest son, Kilafwa, was known for his mind and was an expert planner. All that was developed in the village came from Kilafwa's sharp mind. The younger son, Kun, was known for his physical strength and his fearlessness. He always won athletic contests when competing against other villages on the island.

One day all of the men of Tafunsak gathered for their monthly competition. The events were to take place from morning until sunset. That day, the mother, Sepe, went to a channel by the sea at a place called Saolung. She did not know that the king was passing that way, and so when the king's canoe passed by her, she did not bow her head. The king felt insulted by the woman and so his servants leaped from their canoes and killed the poor woman on the spot.

News of the cruelty of the king was sent to Kilafwa and Kun. The boys promised that they would avenge the death of their mother by killing the king and his servants. Kilafwa, the planner, thought of a way to slay the king by using the strength of Kun. At the narrow channel in the Innem River leading to Lelu they would trick the king by offering him coconuts so that his canoes would stop. The brothers hurried to the channel and waited. Soon the king came and Kilafwa bowed as he stood on the shore with a large basket of coconuts. The king stopped and ordered him to load the coconuts into his canoes. When everyone was looking toward Kilafwa, the youngest brother, Kun, came from the other side of the channel, overturned the canoes, and killed the king and his soldiers.

The brothers were aware that when news of the king's death

*Kun and Kilafwa of Kosrae*

reached his palace, they would be hunted and killed when found, so the boys went high into a mountain with a dog. They killed the animal and made a stone oven, an *um,* in which to cook the dog. They did not want the king's servants to take credit for their death, so they decided to die together by themselves. They held hands and leaped to their deaths from a high cliff in the mountains.

The site where the brothers last stayed is still known by many people in Tafunsak, and is considered to be sacred by some. And people say that the charcoal and the stones from the *um* made for their last meal can still be found today.

## HOW A CHANNEL WAS FORMED ON KOSRAE

There is a channel most of the way around Kosrae that is used today for many purposes such as traveling by people from place to place for social gatherings to bring food from the mountains, and to tow logs used for building houses. The channel was originally made by a large snake while searching for her daughter who had disappeared.

One day the king of the island went to visit his granddaughter on the opposite end of Kosrae. As he came to the harbor of Okat, he saw a beautiful girl swimming nearby. He ordered his servants to capture the girl and take her with them. They picked her out of the water and sailed to the king's palace.

After awhile, the girl's mother, who was a large snake, became worried about her daughter. The girl had been gone for more than two days. The snake left her home and slid to the south, but the girl was not there. Then she went to the west, but she was not there either, nor was she to the north or east when the snake went in those directions. Finally, she came to the village of Lelu. Everywhere that the snake had traveled, she gorged out a big channel in her track that we see as the channel around Kosrae today.

When the snake entered the Lelu Harbor, she crawled beside a rock under a boathouse to rest. The next morning when one of the king's servants was throwing garbage away, he saw the big snake leaning her head on a rock. He hurried back to the palace and the first person he met was the girl. The servant told her about the snake. She knew it was her mother and so she begged the servant to keep silent about what he had seen, and he agreed to not tell anyone. That night, the girl went to her mother and told her to crawl to the king's palace and hide herself in the rafters in the ceiling. By morning, after working all night, the snake-mother of the girl was well concealed.

One day a servant was walking beside the king's court when he heard a strange noise. He looked all around, but could not find its source. He began to walk away when he again heard the unfamiliar noise at the top of the house. When he spotted the snake he could hardly believe his eyes. He then quickly ran off to report to the king what he had seen.

The king suspected that the snake was the lovely girl's mother and that she would take her away when she could. So he ordered all of the women to go to the Innem River to wash clothes. While the women were away, he ordered his men to surround the house where the snake was hiding and to set fire to it. As the house burned, ashes from the fire carried by the wind floated down onto the lap of the girl. When she saw the ashes, she knew what was happening and hurried back to the king's palace.

By the time the girl arrived at the palace, her mother had been burned to death. As the girl cried, she leaped into the fire to die with her mother, and she too was burned to death. The only thing left as a reminder of this sad story is the irregular channel made by the mother-snake while searching for her beautiful daughter long ago.

# Marshall Islands

## WHY SHARKS INHABIT LOWAKALLE REEF

Before the foreigners came to the Marshall Islands there lived a man called Lowakalle on Arno Atoll. He is remembered as a very big and strong man and a fearful fighter.

One day Lowakalle left his people and went to live alone on an isolated islet called Ijoen. No one would visit him because he had warned all of the people to stay away. A long time passed and Lowakalle was nearly forgotten. In fact, his people did not even know if he was dead or alive. Those who passed Ijoen saw no trace of Lowakalle, but no one dared to go ashore.

Later on, the people of Arno bagan to complain about a stranger who visited each village, stealing their most precious possessions. No one knew how the stranger got to each village as there was no sign of footprints or a means of transportation. Then they remembered the mysterious Lowakalle, and began to suspect that it was he who was the thief. And they were right. Lowakalle would raid villages both day and night, and the way he would travel was by swimming. The people could not find a way of stopping him on the land as he was so very strong and powerful.

Then Lowakalle began his worst crimes. From his isolated island he would watch for cooking fires. He would then swim to the smoke, take all of the food, and kill anyone who got in his way. The people were terrified, but Lowakalle could not be stopped.

The situation was desperate, and so a meeting was called of the leaders of all of the villages. They had all suffered gravely and tried to figure a way of destroying Lowakalle. After much discussion, they decided that the only way to eliminate the monster, as they called him, was by deception. They would use Lowakalle's greed against him. After three weeks, everything was prepared. Many canoes set out for the best fishing ground of Arno. After arriving, they caught many fish. They then cut all of their catch into pieces and scattered the intestines about the area. This attracted many sharks.

Lowakalle, meanwhile, watched the fleet from his distant home. When he decided that many fish were being caught, he began to swim toward the area to steal them. Because he was so greedy, he swam very rapidly, right into the center of the sharks. They attacked Lowakalle, and he was killed and eaten.

The fishermen then returned home happily to spread the news that Lowakalle had been killed. The people of Arno felt safe again. To honor the event they named the reef where he was killed Lowakalle, and it has this name to this day.

## WHY PEOPLE AVOID ADRIE AT KWAJALEIN

On a tiny islet of Kwajalein Atoll is a place called Adrie, which means clam shell in Marshallese. No one is permitted to swim in the area because of the ever-present sharks.

On a small islet called Ebadon lived an old woman named Likidudu with her four children. Also on this islet lived a demon who was always hidden in the bushes. The old woman knew about the demon, but she did not want to alarm her children by telling them about the monster. Instead, she told her children that they could play anywhere that they wanted to, but they were forbidden to play near the bushes where the demon was hiding.

The old woman's children were obedient, and so they stayed away from the bushes. But as time passed, they became more and more curious about the forbidden area. So, early one morning, one of the children asked the others to come with him to explore the bushes. They all agreed, left their mats, and wandered into the forbidden area.

After walking for awhile they came upon a small house and went inside. They played there for a long time since it was unoccupied. Eventually the demon appeared, but the children knew no fear of this strange creature, so they continued to play. They even teased the demon and made fun of his strange looks. This made the demon very angry, and he called for the mother, Likidudu. He shouted that he was offended because the children said his arms looked like *nok*, which are sticks from coconut fronds, and his legs looked like *kad*, a string made from coconut husks. They also said that his stomach was so big that they could burst it by stepping on it.

Likidudu quickly took her children home for fear of the angry demon. Then she scolded them for their disobedience and told them to never go near the bushes again. But the children were mischievous and they became bored. One day when their mother was not watching they returned to the demon's house to play and to tease him. They went to the bushes often, and each time the old woman had to fetch them and bring them home.

The children became bolder and bolder and returned to the forbidden area frequently to tease the demon. Then one day the demon became so infuriated that he swallowed the children in one giant gulp. He then called the mother and pretended the children were in his area, but when she came near she could not hear them and knew that something dreadful had happened. So she grabbed the demon and they began to fight. They fought from the demon's house to the far end of the island where a large clam shell was lying on the ground. Finally, Likidudu lifted the demon and smashed him against the clam shell, killing him. She then cut open his stomach and freed her four children unharmed. After cutting the demon into pieces, she threw the parts of his body into the sea. The blood of the demon attracted many sharks to the area.

The place of the clam shell, Adrie, had no sharks before this incident occurred. Today, however, Marshallese stay away from the waters off of Adrie because of the old woman who saved her disobedient children from death, and threw the demon into the sea.

## HOW REEFS WERE FORMED ON MAJURO

A man named Letao on Majuro is famous in the Marshall Islands for his strength, but especially for his tricks and practical jokes that he played on others.

At one time Letao admired the canoe of a king and made a plan to trade for it. He decided to build an attractive, but useless, canoe and fool the king into thinking that the canoe of Letao was superior to that of the king.

A beautiful wood that is strong and shines called *kone* wood is unique because it will not float. Letao built his attractive canoe from this wood and shined and decorated it. Then he went to visit the king of Laura and offered to exchange canoes. The king said that he would come to look at the canoe on the following morning.

When the sun set, Letao pulled his canoe to the shoreline. At low tide, he piled a number of large stones at a place offshore, and dragged his canoe on top of them. Thus, in the morning, when the king arrived, the canoe of Letao appeared to be floating on the surface of the lagoon.

The king was impressed with the appearance of Letao's canoe and did not even consider if it was seaworthy or not. So he gave up his proven craft in exchange for a canoe he had never sailed. Letao hurried away, leaving the king ashore admiring his new boat. He sailed quickly toward the pass leading to the open sea.

The king waded out into the lagoon and boarded his new craft, but when he tried to paddle away, his canoe would not move. He paddled harder, and suddenly his craft was pushed from the rocks, sank, and rested on the bottom of the lagoon.

The king, soaking wet and furious, yelled for his subjects to pursue and capture the tricky Letao. As canoes raced after Letao, he was laughing and singing. As his pursuers closed in, Letao kicked up sand and coral from the bottom of the lagoon. This caused the reefs to form that blocked their way. Still laughing and singing, Letao was last seen sailing into the sea beyond Majuro.

If one visits Majuro today, most people can tell stories of the popular Letao. And the reefs and sandbars in the lagoon are evidence that the story of Letao and the *kone* wood canoe is true.

## HOW A LARGE POOL WAS FORMED ON MEJIT

There are only two pieces of land that are not atolls in the Ratak Chain of the Marshalls, Jimo which is uninhabited, and Mejit, on which people live. On Mejit there is a very big pond in the center of the island that people say was made by a monster a long time ago. At that time there were only two inhabitants there, an old man and his wife. Each evening the old man would go to the center of the island to make copra, and he would remain there into the night. His wife would stay at their home preparing food. One night while away from home, the old man saw something shining in the distance, but he did not go to investigate to see what it was.

The next night the old man returned to his place of work in the middle of Mejit. He suddenly realized that the shining area had become larger, and that it was a pond reflecting moonlight. He returned home to tell his wife that he was going to spend the whole night there to see what was happening. The next evening, his wife prepared food and the old man left to visit the pond.

During the night he noticed that someone or something was working to make the pool larger. He returned to the area several more nights and watched. Then one night he realized that it was a monster working on the pond, and the old man, very much afraid, hurried home to tell his wife. They realized that their lives were in danger from the monster, so they made a plan to slay it before the monster killed them. The man would lure the monster away from the pond, and his wife would entice the monster into their house.

    The old man went to the pond for a final visit. When he saw the creature leave the water, he threw stones to attract him. When the monster chased the old man, they ran towards the house where his wife was standing in the doorway. The old man went quickly inside, hid, and waited. When the monster saw the old lady, he ran into the house after her, and was stabbed in the back and killed with a spear by the old man who was hiding behind the front door.

    Today the island of Mejit is peaceful and the monster is just a memory. His pond, though, is in the center of the island and is enjoyed as a swimming place by all of the people.

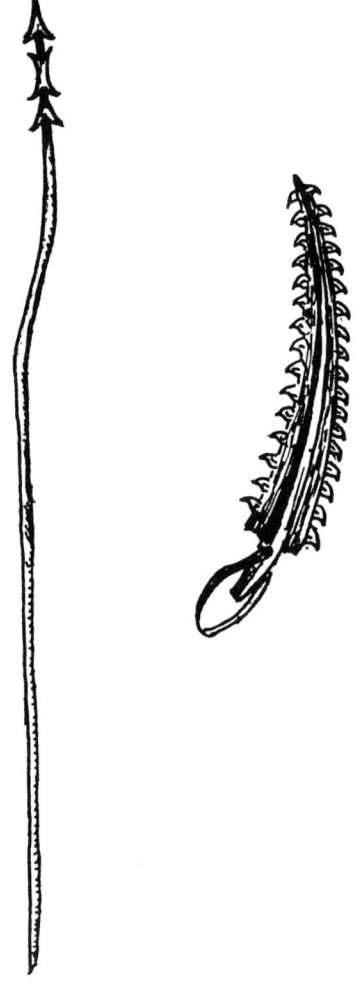

# III.
# Stories of Customs, Skills and Values

*Marshallese Sailing Canoe*

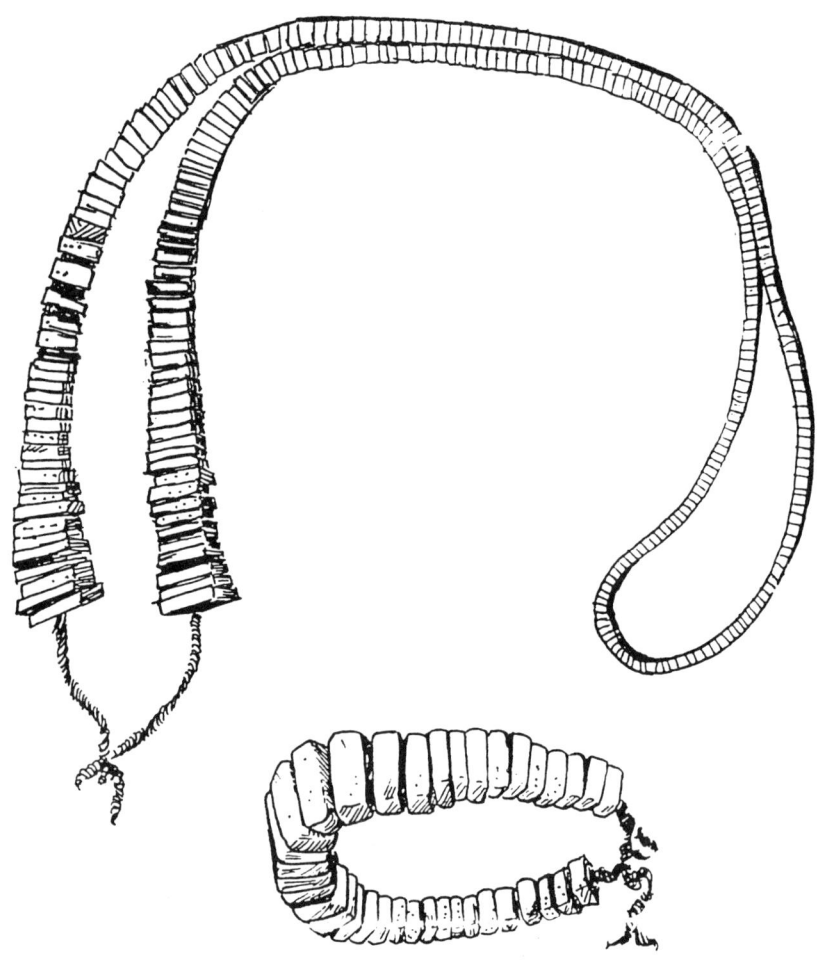

Palauan Stone Jewelry

# *Palau Islands*

## WHY A GIRL BECAME A DUGONG

    Once there lived an old man and his wife. One day the woman went to her taro patch while her husband remained at home. While she was away, the husband was turned into a nut tree by an evil spirit. When his wife returned from her work, her husband was nowhere to be seen. She called and called for him, but could get no answer. She knew something strange must have happened and so she called the names of all the plants nearby hoping for a response. She called the lemon tree, the banana tree, the pineapple plants, the breadfruit tree and many others, but nothing responded to her voice.

    The wife sat down to rest. Then she glanced at the nut tree and remembered that she had not called to it. So she gathered all of her strength and shouted loudly to the nut tree. The strength of her voice caused a branch of the tree to bow, and blood dripped down from it. The wife cried, because she knew her husband had been turned into that tree.

    So the lady remained alone. Then one day she felt a stirring in her womb and knew that she was pregnant. Soon she delivered a very lovely baby girl. As the girl grew up, she asked about her father. Her mother said that he had died long ago and not to worry about him.

    The lady treated her daughter kindly and the girl was very obedient. The mother fed the girl all of the foods available, but told her that she must never eat the nuts from the nearby tree. The girl obeyed her mother's wishes.

One day when the mother had gone to the taro patch, the girl became awfully curious about the nut tree. So while her mother busily cleared the taro patch, the girl picked nuts from the tree and cracked them. When she was about to eat the nuts, her mother suddenly appeared. The girl was ashamed for disobeying her mother so she quickly put the nuts in her mouth to hide them and ran toward the sea. Her mother saw this and followed, begging her daughter not to swallow the nuts. When she reached the shore, the daughter continued running right into the sea and was turned into a *dugong,* a seacow, and disappeared.

The girl had the nuts in her mouth but had not swallowed them when she turned into the creature. Today one can see a bulging in the jaws of the *dugong* where the nuts were in the girl's mouth. When one is caught, it breathes like a human, and when it is about to be killed, one can see tears of the crying daughter flowing from the eyes of the *dugong.*

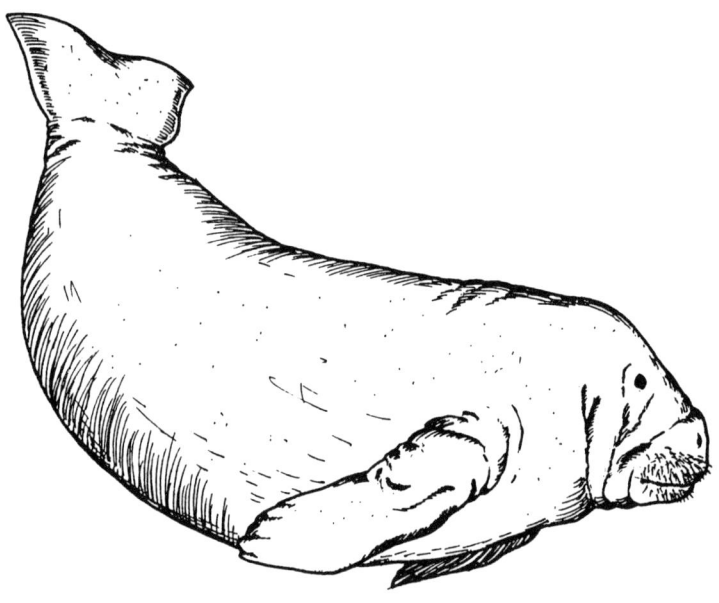

*Dugong*

## WHY BATS AND RATS ARE ALIKE

In the islands of Palau there are many rats. There are also a large number of bats. At one time the rats and the bats always stayed together, but today they are never seen with each other.

One particular rat and bat were very close friends a long time ago, and always played together. But in gathering food, the bat had an advantage because he could fly off and get mango fruit for himself and his rat friend. This was their favorite food.

One day the rat decided to trick his bat friend and take the wings for himself. So the next day the rat asked his friend what it was like to fly around and be able to eat mango at any time. The bat bragged to him that it was wonderful and glorious to have wings. So the rat asked if he could just try on the wings once and see for himself. The bat felt that they were very good friends and so he let the rat borrow the wings. The rat immediately flew high into the sky. As he flew away and looked down, he felt so good, and everything was so beautiful, that he forgot his bat friend and flew away, never to return.

The bat was sad and cried because he was wingless. He took on the habits and characteristics of the rat and had to scurry around to find his food on the ground. And this story explains why today that rats and bats look alike. It is because of an unfaithful friend rat who fooled the bat into parting with his wings.

## WHY PREGNANT WOMEN RECEIVE SPECIAL CARE

Expectant mothers in the Palau Islands always receive special care and consideration. In the past, however, this was not true, as little was known about taking care of pregnant women.

Because there was little knowledge of childbirth methods years ago, women were left pretty much alone during pregnancy. Then, before delivery, a pregnant woman would be operated upon and the infant would be pulled from the mother's womb. Many times women would die from this operation.

It happened that a woman on Babelthaup, the largest island in Palau, became pregnant. As her ninth month of pregnancy approached, she began weeping because she thought she would have to submit to an operation and die. A very kind spirit heard her weeping, felt sorry for her, and decided to give her help. The spirit knew that women were operated on when they first began moaning with labor pains. The spirit came to the woman and advised her to remain silent despite her pain. Women were taken to a special house for the operation. If the expectant mother made no noise, she would not be taken away. The woman did as she was told and remained silent when she felt labor pains.

After some time, the people outside of the house heard the crying of a baby instead of the moans of the woman. When they rushed in they found the mother and child alive and well.

From that time until the present, women have been given great care during pregnancy by friends, and especially relatives, and it is the custom for women to do their best to avoid showing pain in childbirth by moaning and groaning.

# *Yap Islands*

## HOW NET FISHING WAS LEARNED AT GAGIL

Many centuries ago there lived a family in a village called Riken on Gagil Island. The family consisted of the father, Falaragrong, his wife, and a son named Guwol. One day Falaragrong decided to go on a journey, and he called his son to speak to him. He told the boy not to use his fishing equipment while he was away on the trip, but like some children who did not obey their parents, Guwol ignored his father's wishes. One day he decided to go fishing and so he took his father's favorite fishing line. At that time there were no metal fish hooks; they were made from shells. The hook on this particular line was made from turtle shell and was highly prized by Falaragrong.

With his father's line and best hook, the boy went fishing. Soon he hooked a very large fish and he pulled and pulled until the line snapped. The fish then swam away with Falaragrong's hook in its mouth.

A few days later, Guwol's father returned from his trip. When the boy told him what had happened, the father became very upset. He told his son to search for the hook until he found it. Otherwise, the father would leave again and not return at all.

The boy did not know what to do and was feeling very sad. He went alone and sat on a rock by a well and began to cry. Just then two fish emerged from the well by which Guwol was sitting. When they left the well they turned themselves into young girls, and sat with Guwol. He offered them betelnut which they accepted. They asked him why he was upset, and the boy told them his story. Guwol then asked why the girls were in the well, and the girls said that they were there to get fresh water for their father who had a hook caught in his throat. Guwol asked if he could accompany them to their home, and the girls said that he could. They all then swam off together to a very deep ocean area where they dived to the home of the girls' father. And from that time onward, particular fish in the waters of Yap have a red-stained mouth from the betelnut chewed by the girls.

There were all sorts of different fish at the home of the father, and great activity was taking place. They were all trying to find ways of removing the hook from his throat. Finally a group of fish made the father laugh, and the hook popped out of his throat. It turned out to be the one lost by Guwol when his father was away. The girls gave the hook to him and invited him to stay on with them. Their father was the king fish of the area.

Guwol appreciated the invitation and decided to stay at their home under the sea. A method of fishing was used that was only known in that particular area, and this consisted of fishing with a net. The girls who, of course, had become fish again, taught this method to him. They even gave him a new name and he was called Gathangthang.

After staying under the sea for a number of years, he decided to return home. By then he had grown to be a man. So he swam to the surface and returned to the people of Gagil. All of them were surprised and happy to see him, especially his father who got his favorite hook back. The father then forgave his son.

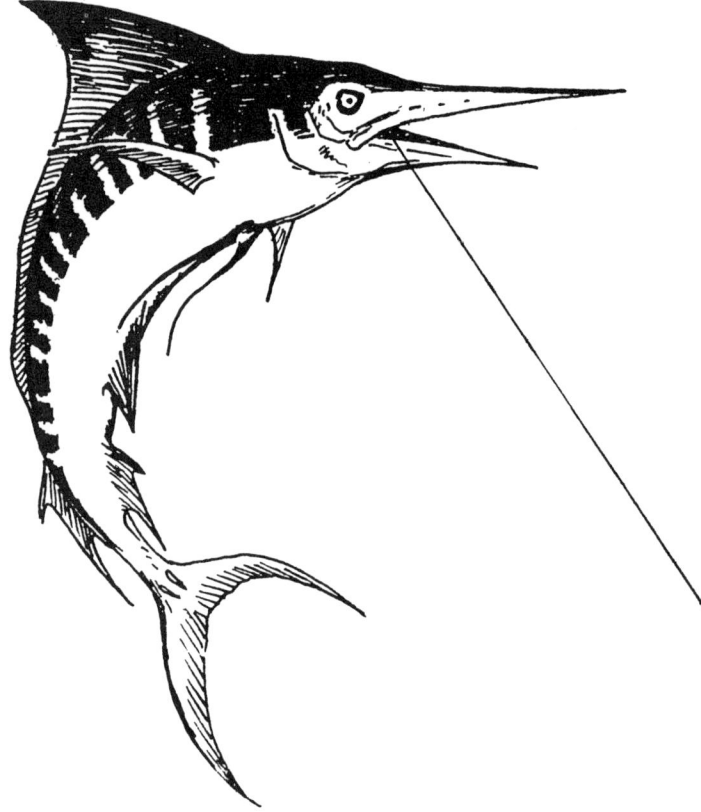

Guwol was happy to be with his people again, and so he taught them all about this new way of net fishing which he had learned. It is called *athing* in Yapese, and has been used throughout the islands ever since.

## HOW OBEDIENCE SAVED A VOYAGE

Once there lived an old couple in Yap who had two sons. The older son was named Rongolap and his younger brother was named Rongoschig. Both parents were very good to their sons, and the father happened to be an exceptional navigator. He patiently taught his sons the art of navigation and both Rongolap and Rongoschig learned this skill quickly and thoroughly.

One day Rongolap felt he was prepared to set sail for another island. He asked his father if he could go on a journey, and his father agreed to let him go. Rongolap, in selecting a crew for his voyage, foolishly chose only young men.

Before sailing, his father gave Rongolap advice that he must be sure to follow. He told him that soon after he set sail he would see an old woman sitting on the reef and fishing. He told Rongolap to be sure to stop and give food to the old woman before he continued his voyage. Then the father told his son that four rocks would appear in the water. When the first rock is approached, all of the crew should remain seated. At the second rock, all should stand up, and at the third rock, the men should take their hats off. Finally, at the fourth rock, they should replace their hats. Rongolap agreed to do all that his father instructed.

On the day chosen for Rongolap and his young crewmen to depart, all of the people on the island came to say farewell. After they set sail, they saw the old woman sitting on a reef, just as the father predicted. But instead of stopping and paying respect to the woman by giving her food, they passed her without even pausing. The old woman shouted to the men, as they were disappearing, that they would sail to their deaths because of their lack of respect for older people.

Rongolap and his men soon approached the first rock mentioned by the father. Instead of sitting down, they stood up. They also confused the instructions about what to do when approaching the other three rocks. They simply got everything mixed up.

After sailing for some distance, an island appeared on the horizon and the men quickly approached it. Rongolap and his crew did not know that this particular island was inhabited by ghosts who ate people. After anchoring, the ghosts, disguised as human beings, offered to clean the canoe. When the ghosts completed this work, Rongolap and his young crew were led to two ponds. One of the ponds was very murky and the other clear and clean. The men immediately began to bathe in the clean pool, and after they were clean they felt weak and went to sleep. It was then that the ghosts made a good meal of Rongolap and his men.

Rongoschig's father and his other relatives patiently waited for his return. Finally, they decided that something terrible must have happened, and Rongoschig decided to trace the route of his lost brother. In selecting his crew, however, Rongoschig selected older men rather than young men as his brother had done. Rongoschig was also given the same instructions by his father and he obeyed them thoroughly.

After passing the old lady and giving food as a sign of respect, and complying with instructions when they passed the four rocks, Rongoschig arrived at the same island where his brother had been eaten. When they went ashore, however, they refused to allow the ghosts to clean their canoe. And when they were led to the same two ponds, they chose to bathe in the murky one. After that, they all felt stronger. Then they all took coconut milk and put it on their faces.

The ghosts waited impatiently for Rongoschig and his men to fall asleep. But morning came and the men were still awake and alert. They then sailed safely back to their home island.

Rongolap did not heed his father's advice and also chose to sail with young men, rather than with an older experienced crew. As a result, he was eaten by ghosts. Rongoschig, however, took his father's advice, and he wisely selected an older crew. As a result, he had no trouble on his voyage and arrived safely home to his people.

# Yap Outliers

## HOW TRAP FISHING WAS LEARNED ON OLIMARAO

Long ago, on the island of Olimarao in Yap State, there lived an old man and his three sons. The boys were very faithful and respectable to their father. At that time, the people of Olimarao were wonderfully skilled in fishing, canoe building, navigation, and even foretelling the future. The old father of the boys was exceptionally good at these skills, but his sons were not aware of this.

One night the sons were called by their father to sit with him on his mat. The brothers were quite surprised because they had never been asked to sit with their father in this manner. They sat a number of minutes in respectful silence, and then their father spoke to them. He told his sons that he loved them and believed they could be good to everyone on the island. He said that this time of the year was the most suitable for learning, and he would start teaching them so they could some day teach all that they knew and share their knowledge with the other people on the island.

The brothers were very happy and delighted that their father was going to teach them. They tried very hard and followed all of the old man's instructions. Soon they could make good fishing traps for themselves and even build small canoes.

One day the brothers asked their father to show them the best place for fishing. The old man smiled and said that he would be glad to do this because they were now responsible young men. He told his sons to bring two coconut fronds to him and they quickly obeyed. Then the old man began talking to the fronds while separating them into four parts. He also tied some strange knots in them. Then he told his sons to accompany him to a place where they had fished before without success, and they put their traps into the water.

The next day the three brothers returned to the area and checked their traps. They were amazed to find them bulged with fish. Every time, in fact, that the old man used his magic words with the fronds, he could predict whether fish would be in the traps or not. If he said there would be none, then there would not be any; if he said the traps were full, then the sons would find many fish.

The three brothers wondered about their father's magic and decided to test it. One day they took their trap to the fishing area, as usual, but instead of putting it under water, they placed it in a tree along the shore. Then they returned home. Two weeks passed and the sons asked their father to again perform magic. The old man was given the fronds, he separated them again, and talked to them. Suddenly he jumped up excitedly and told his sons that he must accompany them to their trap because it was exceptionally full of fish. When he asked his sons where they had laid their trap, the father was told that it was in a tree. But when they all went to the place, they found the trap in the water. It had fallen from the tree into the ocean. Also, it was so filled with fish that the brothers had to ask other men in the village to help them carry their catch.

From then on the three sons never doubted their father. They asked the old man to share his secret of magic with them and he obliged. When the old man died, the three brothers spread the magic throughout the island and even to neighboring islands so others could be helped with their fishing. As a result, today on many islands in Yap State this magic is still commonly used in catching fish.

## HOW FALALEP WAS CAPTURED BY LOSIEP

In the islets of Ulithi Atoll there is a tiny piece of land called Losiep. It is located far from most other islets. Because of its small size, Losiep became over-populated, and even feeding everyone became a problem.

One day the chief of Losiep called a meeting to discuss the problem with his people. It was decided that they should seek another larger island on which the people could live. After much thought, the larger island of Falalep directly to the north was decided upon, but Falalep was already occupied by other people.

The men of Losiep argued and discussed for a whole month about ways to take Falalep. They finally decided to trick the people who were there. The men of Losiep went diving in the sea and collected many large clams. Then they took the clams as a gift to the islanders of Falalep and offered them for a feast. They told the people to leave all of the shells piled on the beach so that it would be easy to discard them later. After the unsuspecting people had eaten very much clam meat, they left the shells on the beach and slept. But the men of Losiep only pretended to sleep and remained awake. Then, early in the morning just before dawn, they came with their slings and shot the empty clam shells like cannon balls at the people of Falalep. Many were killed, and the few survivors tried to escape by swimming away. The people of Losiep then took over Falalep, and have occupied the island ever since.

# *Truk Islands*

## WHY SHARKS ARE FEARED ON TOL

The Trukese people have many myths and legends that have been passed down through the years. These stories often vary from island to island, and one of them is about a lady who had two sharks for babies. It also tells why people fear sharks.

This lady lived in the village of Unifei on Tol. She had been told

by her mother to avoid going to certain places in the village because they were dangerous. Also, there happened to be a pool near the sea where she would bathe and her mother told her to never face the sea while she was taking a bath. It happened that while she was bathing one day when she was pregnant, she faced the sea and suddenly felt that she was going to deliver. But what came out of her womb were twin sharks, and they quickly swam away into the sea. With a sorrowful heart, the lady returned home and told her mother what had happened and they both wept. The girl knew that she had disobeyed the wishes of her mother.

The lady would often return to the pool where her sharks would be waiting for her. Time passed on, and one day the lady went fishing with her niece. She felt very hungry and she asked the young girl to get food from her brothers. When the girl went for the food, she was told that none was cooked and to wait a few hours. The niece misunderstood the message and told the lady that her relatives would not give her any food. The lady, of course, felt extremely sad thinking that her brothers had neglected her, and she decided to run away from home.

At this time, there was a sailing ship at the village ready to leave. The lady decided to sneak aboard the ship and hide herself. She did this, and the ship left the island. While at sea, a terrible storm struck and nearly capsized the ship. The crew knew that something must be wrong and they searched the craft and found the lady. It was known to be bad luck at that time to have a woman aboard, and so the men threw the lady overboard to drown.

The lady swam until she was exhausted, and then she called for her twin shark sons to get her home. After they safely returned her to Unifei, the lady told the sharks to go to the ship and destroy it. They did as they were told and sank it. Then, they ate all the people except for the old man who had tried to help the lady. As a result of this incident, sharks today have an appetite for people, and humans are careful to avoid them.

# *Truk Outliers*

## WHY THE ISLET OF AMES WAS DESTROYED

Things can be seen in a certain form today, and how they came

*The Stories of Customs, Skills and Values* — 103

to be this way is often recorded in stories told on Namoluk Atoll. The atoll is much smaller today than it was in the past, and a story is told about how part of it was destroyed and became uninhabited.

Upon the arrival of the first Christian missionaries, Namoluk consisted of two inhabited islands called Ames and Namoluk. However, something unusual happened that eliminated the people from Ames and caused it to be the uninhabited islet that one sees today.

The tragedy all began when a German missionary brought a minister from another island to preach more to the people about the Bible and God. However, it happened that the people of Ames did not appreciate someone similar to themselves being their minister. The German missionary was upset, and tried very hard to convince the people that they should accept the new minister. The people still refused to give in. (Perhaps the reason that the natives did not want to accept the outsider was because they thought that he might be a spy. It seems that a certain kind of fish was due to come to their reef in large schools very soon, and it was possible that the outsider had come to Ames to get information.) The German missionary then cast a spell on the people of Ames for not accepting the new minister. He supposedly told them that their island would turn into a place inhabited by creatures other than people.

After the religious people were forced away, a *Langupwis,* one who could predict future events, told of the destruction coming to the island. And it was true. A sickness swept over the whole population except for a few of the inhabitants who managed to escape to neighboring Namoluk. A small remnant of these people remains today, but most of the beautiful people of Ames died from the sickness.

After this, the spell was acknowledged to be true and the island of Ames was then used by the people of Namoluk to raise pigs. But even this did not succeed because a typhoon in 1958 killed all of the animals. Today, Ames is an uninhabited islet in the Namoluk Atoll, and only the birds make noise.

## HOW FISHING METHODS WERE LEARNED ON LUKUNOR

There is a clan on Oneop Islet on Lukunor Atoll that is known to be great net fishermen. People from this clan are also known to be able to swim among sharks without fear. All of this has resulted from a brother who was unhappy with his three sisters and tried to commit suicide.

The parents of the brother and sisters had died, and as the firstborn, the man was the leader of the family. One day long ago he went to the taro patch to collect food for the family. He returned with a sack full of taro and a small one which he preferred called "tune." After asking his sisters to cook his taro, he fell asleep.

The sisters loved and respected their brother and wondered why he should have such a small and ugly taro. So they changed it with a large delicious one. When the brother awoke and asked for his food, he was given the unfamiliar taro and became very angry. He thought the sisters were playing a trick on him and that they no longer respected him. He was so upset, in fact, that he decided to end his life.

First he attempted suicide by hanging. But people in the community would not leave him alone. Then he decided to walk into the sea after dark and drown. After sunset, he entered the lonely water. He had with him a rope tied around his neck attached to a heavy stone that was floated on a log. He swam beyond the sight of Oneop.

After swimming for some time he spied a large, dark shape ahead which he thought was a whale. Being curious, he swam toward it only to find out that it was an unknown island. He delayed his suicide plan so he could investigate the place.

The man walked to the center of the island where he found an old lady in a hut preparing nine breadfruits for her nine sons. The old lady had massive breasts and could not see because her hair and eyebrows covered her eyes. Every minute the old lady would count her nine breadfruits by touching them with her hands. Suddenly the man grabbed one breadfruit, and the old lady noticed that it was missing when she counted. Helpless to find it, she shouted that she would do a favor for whoever took the breadfruit if it was returned to her. The man then returned it. Suddenly the old lady's nine sons were heard coming home. The old woman told the man to hide to avoid harm. She said that her sons could not see, but their sense of touch was highly developed.

The man searched everywhere for a hiding place but could not find one. The lady knew her sons would touch everything when they suspected a stranger was near, but they would never touch her very large breasts, so she told the man to hide beneath them.

Her sons sensed that someone was near by the unfamiliar odor of the stranger, and they searched everywhere, but to no avail.

Finally they took their breadfruit to their hut, ate it, and went to sleep to be fresh for the night's fishing. The man thanked the old lady, then he cut her hair and her eyebrows and she was thrilled to find she could see again.

The man had given up his idea of killing himself and asked the old lady how he might return home. She said her sons would fish near Oneop that night and that he should accompany them. But she warned him to sit away from the wind so they could not smell him, and to always do the counting when roll was taken.

That night they all sailed toward Oneop, and near the islet they set their fishing nets. The man tied the nets securely to the coral reef without notice, because the nine sons of the old lady could not see. He then left the canoe and swam to Oneop a short distance away. After the net was filled with fish, the nine brothers tried in vain to untie their net, but they were unable to. They could only use their sense of feel and not their sense of sight. Finally, frustrated and angry, the nine brothers left their net and their catch and sailed homeward to avoid the dawn.

When the man arrived on Oneop the people were overjoyed to see him because they thought he had drowned. He told them of his adventures. To prove the story he took the strongest men on Oneop to where the fishing net was placed. There they found it crammed with fish. They shouted in happiness, and so all those left behind knew that the story was true.

# *Pohnpei Island*

## THE FIRST SAKAU ON POHNPEI

In olden times on Pohnpei there lived a man named Uitenegar. He prayed all of the time to the god Luk, and had sacrificed all offerings to him from the time of his youth. When Uitenegar was old, he could neither see nor walk. Because Uitenegar had always been such a faithful servant to Luk, his prayers reached the god, and one day Luk came to earth to visit Uitenegar.

When Luk arrived, Uitenegar was resting at home and heard a great noise in front of his house. He shouted to find out who was outside and a voice answered that it was Luk making the noise. Uitenegar was disappointed that Luk had waited so long to visit him because now he was old, blind and feeble. When Luk saw this, he transformed Uitenegar into a young man so that he could walk and see things again.

Luk and his servant then traveled to Madolenihmw. They then went further to a place called Tolopwail. There they climbed into the water that carried the stream to the sea and they finally arrived at a place named Rir where they rested.

Because of Luk, Uitenegar was as strong as he had been in his youth and could see once more. Since he was young again, all of the old skin fell from his body and new skin took its place. The skin under his feet also fell away.

Luk took the old skin from under the feet of Uitenegar and buried it. From the skin grew a plant that Polynesians called kava, but all Micronesians know as *sakau*. This made Uitenegar very happy. Luk then took a plant of *sakau* and returned to the sky, and Uitenegar also did not remain in the world any longer.

## A BIRD AND A STOLEN SOUL

Once there was a spirit named Lisotam who stole the soul of a woman on Pohnpei. The spirit snatched the soul and leaped out of a window. As the spirit was leaving, the husband of the woman was arriving. The husband threw a stone at the spirit and hurt the spirit's arm, and made him quite angry. The spirit then held tightly to the soul and flew with it quickly to the west.

Without her soul, the woman became very ill and she lay in her house for many days. Finally, she asked for her clan to gather around her because she felt that she was going to die. The spirit Lisotam had indeed flown away with the soul, and the spirit and the soul were enjoying each other far off in the west.

Then one day a seagull flew near the home of the sick woman who had lost her soul, and the gull landed there. The bird saw the woman was becoming weak, and heard people talking about how her soul had been stolen from her. And so the gull flew west in search of the spirit.

He found the soul and the spirit enjoying the company of each other. The seagull flew straight at the spirit and grabbed the soul and flew away. The seagull flew with the soul until the house was located where the sick woman lay. On this day, the woman was to die. The bird crouched down on the doorstep and entered the house quietly.

The bird went close to the woman and lay her soul on her head with its beak. The sick woman, with her soul returned, quickly became healthy again, and her entire clan celebrated.

## HOW DECEPTION SAVED U

Isokelekel is known in Pohnpeian legend as a fierce warrior who came to the island from Katau many years ago. He captured Nan Madol, which was the capital of Pohnpei at the time, and then set out to defeat all of the tribes on the island. He took his canoe and 333 men and began his conquest.

There was a warrior of giant size named Taukataur living at U. He was such a large man that he had to bend over when speaking to people. Because of his large size, he was greatly respected and considered to be the protector of the people of U. Also, he possessed magic powers. His home was under a rock at Awak.

Isokelekel and his companions first sailed to Saladak in U and started to land, but suddenly saw Taukataur standing on the shore holding a huge club and wearing a yellow grass skirt. Isokelekel feared that the men of Saladak were all as large as this man with the yellow grass skirt, and so he sailed on to find an easier enemy.

*Taukataur of U*

Taukataur immediately hurried down the coast ahead of Isokelekel. When the canoe again tried to land at U, they saw a very large warrior holding a club and wearing a blue grass skirt. Since the skirt was a different color, Isokelekel did not know that this warrior was the same Taukataur. Fearing that these men also were too large to defeat, he sailed without landing again.

Taukataur again moved away quickly to Awak, where Isokelekel was headed. By magic, he changed his grass skirt to a red color this time. When Isokelekel again saw the large warrior, he did not know that he was the same Taukataur and he again sailed on without landing. Because of Taukataur's deception, Isokelekel did not set foot on the soil of U.

Isokelekel eventually captured most of Pohnpei Island. Without the courage, deception and magic of Taukataur, however, he would have added the people of U to his domain.

## HOW POHNPEI WAS CONQUERED

Every Pohnpeian knows the name Isokelekel, and the story of how he became the first traditional leader, or *Nahnmwarki*, of Pohnpei.

Many years ago, the island was ruled by cruel, tyrannical kings called *Saudeleurs*. The last *Saudeleur* of Pohnpei imprisoned the thunder-god, Nansapwe, for roaring too much and too loudly. But Nansapwe was able to escape and sail on his canoe eastward toward Katau, which is now called Kosrae. Enroute, however, his canoe started to sink and he was only saved by a needle fish who skimmed him over the waves to the island.

On Katau, Nansapwe met a woman named Lipanmai who was a member of his clan, the Under the Breadfruit Clan. He provided her with a bitter piece of fruit which she ate. She then became pregnant. Later she bore a son whom she named Isokelekel. When still a youth, the boy always heard stories of the cruel *Saudeleurs* of Pohnpei, and when he grew up he decided to avenge the treatment of his relative Nansapwe by conquering Pohnpei.

Isokelekel sailed for Pohnpei with 333 men. He first landed at Ant, and then after a while sailed to Madolenihmw. Isokelekel and his group were allowed ashore, although the *Saudeleur* did not trust their intentions as being peaceful. Isokelekel acted as a common traveler so he could learn more about Pohnpeians without it being obvious what he was doing. A lieutenant of Isokelekel's, Nahnesen, helped the leader plan the strategy to defeat the men of the *Saudeleur*.

No one is sure how the actual conflict started, but the men from Katau and those from Pohnpei began battling at Nan Madol. The Pohnpeians were pushing Isokelekel's men back toward the sea with their reckless attacks. When a Pohnpeian named Taukir wounded Isokelekel with a rock from a sling, the leader began to fight furiously, but still the invaders from Katau were retreating. Finally, in desperation, Nahnesen rammed his spear through his own foot and yelled that he would fall back no further! This brave deed inspired his men so much that they fought desperately and won the battle. The *Saudeleur* was chased into the Senpehn River where he became a fish called *Palaiaw* that to this day is not eaten by Pohnpeians.

When the war ended, the victors did not punish those they had defeated. In fact, Isokelekel even rewarded the young soldier who had wounded him by giving him a traditional title and a piece of land. Isokelekel then became the first traditional leader that we know

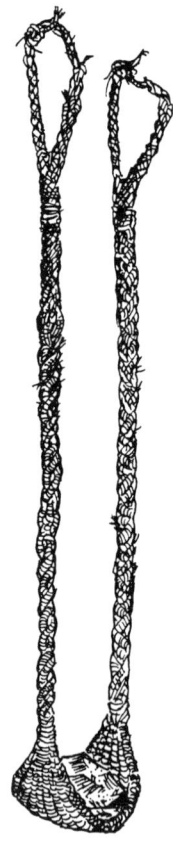

today, the *Nahnmwarki*, of the island. He appointed his son to be the first *Nahnken*, a title that is nearly as high as the *Nahnmwarki* today.

## AN UNGRATEFUL BOY AND A TURTLE

Once on Pohnpei there lived a boy who liked to climb trees and catch birds. On a particular day he took the birds he had caught, along with a ripe coconut to eat, and went to the reef. There he met a friendly turtle. The boy asked the turtle to give him a ride to the land from which he had come, and the turtle agreed to take him. So the boy released his captive birds and climbed on the shell and the turtle swam away with him.

The boy and the turtle traveled for a long distance to a faraway place. When the boy became hungry, he asked the turtle if he could open his coconut by cracking it on the turtle's hard shell. The turtle said he could, but instead of striking the shell, the boy smashed the coconut on the turtle's head. The turtle became angry and dove under the water, throwing the boy off. When the boy was almost exhausted from swimming and was drowning, the turtle felt sorry for him and let the boy climb again onto his shell.

Swimming further, the boy and the turtle then arrived at a coral reef where the turtle told the boy to climb off. But the boy was afraid to get off the turtle because there were too many shells there. So the turtle took the boy closer to shore to a dry bank on the reef, and again told the boy to climb off of his back. But again the boy refused saying he was afraid of the many crayfish nearby. Then the turtle carried the boy up to a dry beach and asked him to climb off, and the boy finally did so.

The boy, though, was very ungrateful for the help he had been given by the turtle, and he called all of the demons to come and make a meal out of the turtle. All of the demons hurried to the boy and made preparations for the feast. Some gathered stones for the oven, the *uhmw*, and others gathered firewood. Some demons grabbed the turtle and began to cut into his entrails. The turtle begged the demons to stop and told them to take him to a place by the water to remove his entrails so that they wouldn't leave a big mess. The demons agreed, and took the turtle to a place where the water was deep. Suddenly, the turtle slapped the ground with his strong fins and escaped into the deep water. The demons became furious because they had been tricked and had worked so hard to prepare for the feast. So they all began to eat the ungrateful boy while the turtle swam happily away into the deep waters of the sea.

# *Pohnpei Outliers*

## THE FEMALE PEOPLE-EATER OF PAKIN

Some time ago there were two women who lived on islands close to Pohnpei. One lived on Pakin and the other lived on Ant. They were named Lih en Pakin and Lih en Ant. They were friends and would gossip with each other throughout the day. Secretly, however, Lih en Pakin wanted to kill and eat Lih en Ant.

While on Pakin one night, the two women were lying down on a sleeping mat. The woman from Pakin told her friend from Ant something that put her at ease and caused her to sleep. When asleep, she intended to eat her. However, a parrot came to Lih en Ant and warned her to stay alert because her friend wanted to kill her. The parrot advised her to take a coconut shell and divide it in two parts and leave it where she slept. Then she should destroy the canoe of Lih en Pakin and travel rapidly in her own canoe home to Ant.

When Lih en Pakin returned to where her friend should have been asleep, all she found was coconut shells and she became angry. Then the parrot defecated on her and she became furious and ran to her canoe. When she found it in pieces, she climbed a tall palm tree and ordered the tree to grow taller. As it grew higher, she commanded the tree to bend over until it was atop the canoe of the fleeing Lih en Ant.

The parrot had advised the woman from Ant to place a mussel at the end of her canoe and the parrot gave her a very large one. When Lih en Pakin stepped on the back of the canoe, her foot went into the mussel shell. The large shell clamped shut on the leg of Lih en Pakin and both tumbled overboard. The mussel carried the woman to the bottom of the sea where she drowned.

Lih en Ant then sailed safely to her home. It is said that she later became a princess on her island.

## LODUP OF MWOAKILLOA

People of Mwoakilloa have great respect for strong men, and Lodup was one of the strongest ever known. Lodup was a giant of a man who lived with his wife and their two sons. His feats of strength are still famous on the island. He had a taro patch on Kahlap, one of the islets of Mwoakilloa, and it is said that Lodup made this patch by picking up a large stone by himself and throwing it from the middle of Kahlap into the sea.

Another story showing the strength of Lodup is often told. In this story he saved all of the people of Mwoakilloa from a force of invading canoes. It seems that Lodup was sound asleep on the neighboring islet of Mwandohn when the people saw an uncountable number of canoes heading toward Mwoakilloa. The islanders knew that only Lodup could defeat this large enemy, so they hurried to Mwandohn to awaken him. But Lodup had been asleep for fully three weeks and the people were unable to waken him from his slumber. They became so worried that they lost hope, and then they remembered Lodup's bell was made from mountainous stone. They rang the bell two times, shouting Lodup's name twice, and then paused. They did this repeatedly until the huge, strong man began to stir. Finally Lodup was wide awake and saw the fleet of canoes approaching. He grabbed the two tallest coconut trees on the island and pulled them out by their roots without effort. Then he tied each of his sons to one of the trees with coconut fronds and swung them effortlessly over the attacking canoes. As he did this, his sons were able to kill all of the invaders and sink their canoes. The people of Mwoakilloa were then safe and Lodup was respected and admired even more than before.

One day the islanders thought that they might be able to beat Lodup at diving, so they set up a competition. It was decided that everyone would dive into the sea and stay underwater for as long as possible. The last one to surface would win the competition. So the competitors all dived into the lagoon, but Lodup chose to dive into the deep water beyond the reef. When the last man could hold his breath no longer, he surfaced, but Lodup remained submerged. Finally, the people thought that Lodup had drowned and that they had finally beaten him at something, but Lodup was still holding his breath at the bottom of the sea. In fact, he remained there for nearly five years. When he tried to move, he found he was anchored in place by coral that had grown on top of him over the years, and so Lodup drowned. Before he died he shook himself. This caused the whole island to shake and trees to topple and houses to tumble. It also showed to all of the people that it is a mistake to think that they could beat Lodup at anything.

## THE FIRST CHIEF OF PINGELAP

A very long time ago there lived on Pingelap only two women. One was normal like anyone else and had a young son, and the other was a spirit-woman. When the boy would play and run around, his mother told him to always avoid the places where the spirit-woman lived because she was known to eat children.

When the boy grew to maturity, he decided to end the problem once and for all, so he asked his mother to get a spear for him with which to fight the cannibal spirit. His mother got a spear for him, and after a fight, the spirit-woman was killed. Then his mother brought the young man a wooden bowl, and they placed the eyes of the spirit-woman in it and carried it to the reef. There they cast the bowl afloat in the sea.

The bowl drifted for a long distance until it reached the home island of the spirit-woman. The people there knew the eyes to be those of the spirit-woman, so they decided to go to the place from which the wooden bowl had floated away and take their revenge.

The young man who had killed the spirit-woman was watching from a tall palm tree when he saw many canoes approaching Pingelap. There were a hundred in all. He called his mother and told her to fetch a hundred spears for him, which she did. The young man then climbed into a canoe with his spears and sailed out to meet the invaders. In the ocean he killed all of those in the canoes and not a single person survived.

The brave young man then returned to Pingelap and was welcomed back by his mother. Later she had many more children. The first-born son, however, who killed the spirit-woman and saved the island from invasion, is remembered as the first paramount chief of Pingelap.

## WHY COCONUT TREES FLOURISH ON PAINA AT SAPWUAHFIK

There is a small islet called Paina nine miles from the main islet of Ngatik on Sapwuahfik Atoll. The islet was first inhabited by the daughter of a king who was rejected by her parents.

On Ngatik long ago lived a king and queen with a daughter named Limenarleng. In those days women wove skirts and mats from the fronds of coconut palms, and even the queen would go with the village women throughout the island gathering materials for their weaving.

One day Limenarleng was resting on the beach because she was pregnant. The queen brought palm leaves and the king's *tor*, a grass skirt, and left them with Limenarleng to dry in the sun. She told her daughter to look after the leaves and the tor and to be sure that they did not get wet. Then the queen left with the other women, but Limenarleng was drowsy and soon she fell asleep. When she awoke later, the tide had risen and everything was soaking wet.

The king and the queen discovered what had happened and they abused and scolded their pregnant daughter, which is very much against the custom on Ngatik. Then they told her to leave their home. So Limenarleng left Ngatik when the tide was very low and walked toward the beach. Since the tide was out she walked and walked until she reached Paina. She took with her only a single coconut which she planted on her newly-found islet.

Back on Ngatik the king and the queen were melancholy and lonely, for their daughter had been gone many months. They searched everywhere, but Limenarleng was nowhere to be found.

The month of Limenarleng's delivery arrived and she gave birth to a son. When the boy matured and was old enough to sail a canoe, his mother built one for him and told him to sail on to Tgatik and visit his grandparents. Before he left she told him that if the fronds of their coconut palms turned yellow in his absence, then he would know that she had died.

The boy sailed his canoe to Ngatik, but when he arrived, he was beaten by the people and cast into the sea because he did not know the custom of how a strange canoe should approach the island. He was left to drown when an old lady, who happened to be one of the king's maids, came to the shore and rescued him. She then took the boy to her home.

The king and queen very soon discovered that the strange boy was their grandson, for he sang songs about his mother and why he came to Ngatik that only Limenarleng's son could know. All of the people were happy and a royal feast was prepared in the boy's honor.

Soon, the boy told his grandparents that he must return to Paina because his mother was left there alone. So the king and queen prepared to accompany the boy and ordered all of the people to come with them. They all sailed for Paina the next day. When the island was sighted, the boy began to weep, for he saw that the fronds of their trees had turned from green to yellow. He knew that his mother had died. And even today on the small island of Paina, yellow fronds are found as a reminder of Limenarleng and her son.

## WHY FLOUNDER FISH ARE FLAT

A lobster and a flounder fish have certain characteristics. A lobster has long feelers and a flounder is a flat fish. At one time, the flounder was shaped like any other fish, but became flattened by an angry lobster.

The two sea creatures were at one time very good friends and would often play together. One day the lobster suggested to the flounder that they play a game of hide-and-seek. The flounder agreed, and the lobster was the first in the game to try and hide. He crawled into a hole in the coral reef and hid his body, but his feelers remained outside of the hole. When the flounder went to search for his friend, the lobster was very easy to find, and the flounder won the first game.

Then it was the flounder's turn to hide. Rather than swim away and conceal himself, he stirred up a sand cloud on the ocean floor next to the lobster, and hid in the cloud while standing close to his friend. The lobster could see nothing because of the swirling sand, and when the flounder teased the lobster while standing very close to him, and the lobster could not see the flounder, it made the lobster

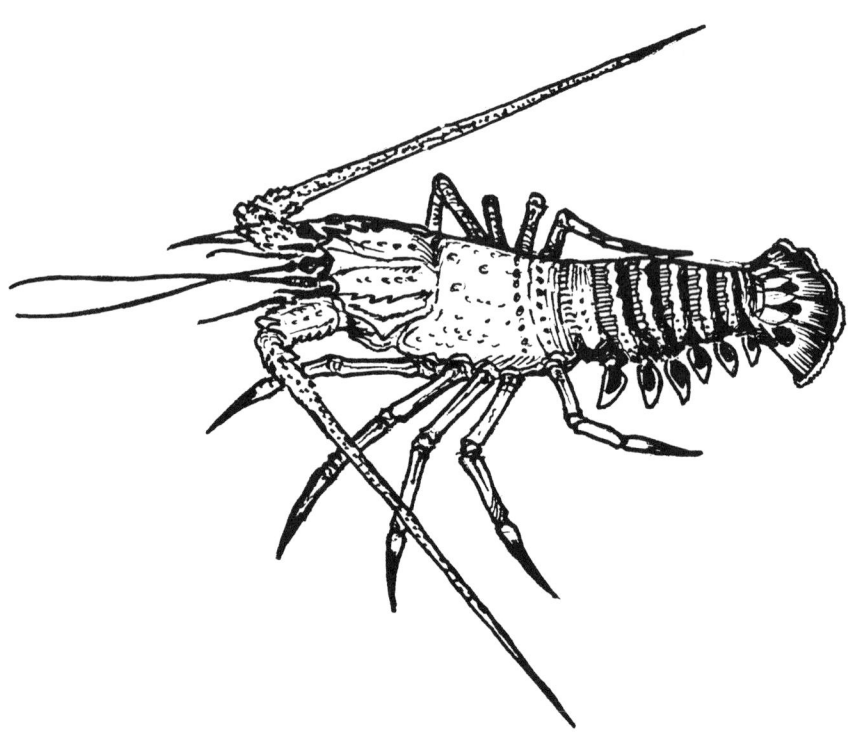

very angry because he had been tricked. When the sand settled, the lobster stomped on the flounder so hard that the fish was flattened out. He then poked out the eye of the flounder and stuck it back on the top of the flounder's head.

Now flounders in the ocean are very hard to see because they lie flat on the sea floor's sand. And the lobsters are quite easy to find because they still have not learned how to conceal their feelers when hiding in the coral rocks.

# *Kosrae Island*

## HOW THE GIANTS WERE KILLED BY NIFOROK

Many years ago on the beautiful island of Kosrae there lived giants as well as ordinary people. These giants controlled the island and were known to be very, very cruel. Whenever they demanded something, the smaller people would have to get what the giants desired. If a person failed to get what a giant wanted, the person would be killed and eaten as punishment for disobeying the giant. As a result of this, the population of Kosrae was decreasing because the people could not get everything that the giants demanded.

In the mountains of Kosrae, far away from the four villages, lived a young and strong man named Niforok. One day he came down from his mountain home and saw an old woman sitting on a rock and crying. When Niforok asked her why she was so sad and weeping, the old woman told him about the terrible giants who often killed and ate people. Niforok became very angry when he heard about this, and decided to try to do something to defeat the giants.

Early the next day Niforok returned to the mountains. There he used powerful magic to try to find a way to kill the giants, and late in the afternoon an idea came to him on how to do this. He then left the mountains to go to the village of Utwe where the king of the giants was known to stay.

Niforok arrived at the town at sunset and collected dead coconut fronds with which he made a torch. He then covered his entire body with clay so that he had a very red appearance. Around midnight, with his lighted torch, he started walking towards the reef, and after a short distance he met the king of the giants.

When the king of the giants saw Niforok's body all red by the torchlight he became very curious and asked how his body became so red. Niforok replied that he had a special skill and could make anyone's body red if he wanted to. This pleased the giant and he commanded Niforok to make his body red the next day. Niforok told the giant he must wait until the day after tomorrow. He said he would then make the bodies of all the giants red at the same time. This made the king of the giants very happy and he agreed to this plan.

Later, when the giants arrived at the home of Niforok, a great *um*, or stone oven, was already prepared. The stones were very hot and as red as the setting sun. To make their bodies red, Niforok told the king of the giants, each giant must be tied to a large coconut tree. The king foolishly agreed to this. Niforok tied each giant to a tree and then took red hot stones from the *um* and put them in the throats of the giants. The king wondered why the giants were struggling, but Niforok reassured him and told him not to worry, that his plan was working just right. At last it was the king's turn and he commanded Niforok to make him red quickly. Niforok then took the largest and the hottest stone from the *um* and shoved it into the throat of the king. In his haste, the king of the giants gulped away his life and all of the giants were dead.

*Kosrae Warrior (circa 1720)*

## HOW UNKINDNESS WAS REPAID ON KOSRAE

There lived a very cruel giant on Kosrae long ago who killed many people. All of the people were so afraid that they decided to leave their homes and escape. So they made barges and began the long, treacherous journey to Pohnpei.

There lived a girl on Kosrae named Nimac who had no one to take her on the trip, so she went to the mouth of the harbor and sat on a rock and waited for a barge to take her to Pohnpei. When the first group of people came, she called and called. As the barge stopped to see what the girl wanted, she asked to be taken with them. The leader of the group told the girl to wait for the next barge. In a few minutes, the next barge approached and the girl called to them and asked to be taken along. The second group also refused to take her. When the third barge came she asked the same question and got the same answer. Finally, the last barge passed her and would not take the girl along with them.

The girl sat still on the rock with tears flowing down her cheeks, heart-broken, as she watched everyone sail away from Kosrae to safety. At last, she picked up a flower and put it behind her ear and went slowly home. She was the only person remaining on the island, except for the giant.

A few weeks later, the girl gave birth to a son. She named him Nepahsr. Years passed and the child grew to be a strong boy. He had always wanted to paddle across the lagoon, so he asked his mother to build a canoe for him. She built a small canoe for her son, but told him never to paddle far away because there was something from which they must hide.

One day the boy paddled too far and reached the home of the giant, but the giant was not there at the time. The boy ate some of the giant's bananas and threw the skins into the sea. He took a rooster, paddled home, and told his mother about his trip. Meanwhile, the skins of the bananas floated until they hit the giant's canoe. The giant then suspected that there must be something wrong and so he paddled home to see what was happening. When he saw his home disturbed, he was furious and began looking for the thief. From his sense of smell he followed the trail to Lelu where he found the boy.

Nepahsr and the giant then fought fiercely for a long time, and the boy finally defeated the giant. This made the mother very happy, and the news spread throughout Micronesia that the giant had been killed. When the Kosraean people on Pohnpei heard the good news, they hurried to return home.

After a short time the boy saw the people returning from Pohnpei, and he told his mother. The mother, though, remembered well how all the people had forsaken her and left her to die. She told her son to climb a very high coconut tree, pick a young coconut, cut it in half, and face it toward the sea. The boy did as he was told and this caused a great typhoon to occur that killed all of the people except for the king and queen. By magic, they were then turned into small fish that eat their own feces.

At a time much later, different people came to populate the island. But all of the people who had been unkind to Nimac were gone from Kosrae forever.

*Kosrae Canoe (early 1800s)*

## WHY CATS HATE DOGS

On top of a hill on Kosrae once stood a beautiful house that is no longer there. It was surrounded by banana and other fruit trees, sugarcane, flowers, and very fertile farmland. To one side, there was a wonderful view of the sunrise and to the other a beautiful view of the sunset.

A couple lived in the house who had a daughter that they called *Kosro* (Dog), and a son named *Kisrik* (Cat). The two children were often together. They worked early every morning on the farmland surrounding their lovely home. In fact, they worked so hard that they resented their parents for forcing them to stay at their labor while others played games and went fishing and swimming.

One day *Kosro* and *Kisrik* made a plan to escape and sneak away from their work in order to play with their friends on the beaches of Kosrae. After they left, their parents went to awaken them as they did each morning, but the children were gone. At that moment, a typhoon suddenly struck and blew everything in its path away. The top of the hill disappeared along with the beautiful home and everything was scattered in the valley below.

After the children were tired from playing, *Kosro* and *Kisrik* left the beach and headed toward their home. It was then that they learned that their home and mother and father had been blown away. From that moment onward, Dog and Cat blamed each other for the tragedy that had taken place. Now, dogs and cats stay away from each other and distrust one another, and frequently fight because of the two disobedient children, *Kosro* and *Kisrik*.

# *Marshall Islands*

## HOW FIRE CAME TO LIKIEP

In the Marshall Islands lived two brothers named Letao and Jamelut. Letao possessed magic powers and he also enjoyed playing tricks on people. This story tells about a trick that Letao played, and about how fire was introduced to the Marshall Islanders.

One day Letao and Jamelut visited Likiep Atoll. After anchoring their canoe in the lagoon, the two brothers went ashore. Letao and Jamelut were very hungry after their journey and they soon saw a group of men line-fishing. Letao asked one of the men if he could borrow a fishing line, but the man told Letao to go find one for himself. He asked the others in the group, but the answer was the same. This made Letao so angry that he used his magic power to turn the men into trees called *kone* in the Marshalls.

Letao and Jamelut wandered further down the beautiful sandy beach of Likiep. Soon they came upon a group of boys who were fishing. When Letao again asked to borrow a fishing line, a boy gave him one. Letao caught many fish. He told the boys to gather some leaves on which to put his catch, and they quickly obliged. He then told the boys that he would do them a favor by teaching them to make fire. The boys thought that this was marvelous because until then people always had to eat raw fish and meat on Likiep.

Letao gathered some leaves and lit a fire. The boys were very surprised. He then told them to gather some rocks, place them in the fire and wait until the rocks became red hot. After this was done, they cooked their fish using the heated stones.

While they were all eating, Letao asked which fish were preferred, the cooked or the raw. All of the boys said that the fish was better cooked. After they ate, Letao made another fire and gave it to the boy whose fishing line he had borrowed. Letao told the boy that it was a gift for being so kind. The boy put some burning sticks and leaves in his *tebteb,* a box used for carrying tools. The boy then quickly ran home with the fire and showed it to his parents. But the parents were afraid of the fire and told the boy to keep it in his *tebteb.*

It was not long before the fire burned through the box. Soon the whole house was ablaze and the boy ran crying from his home. He found Letao and told him that the fire burned down his house, but Letao told the boy he was speaking nonsense. He said for him to return home. The boy did as he was told. When he got home he found his house to be standing and that nothing had happened. Letao had just played another of his famous tricks, and fire was introduced to the people of the Marshall Islands.

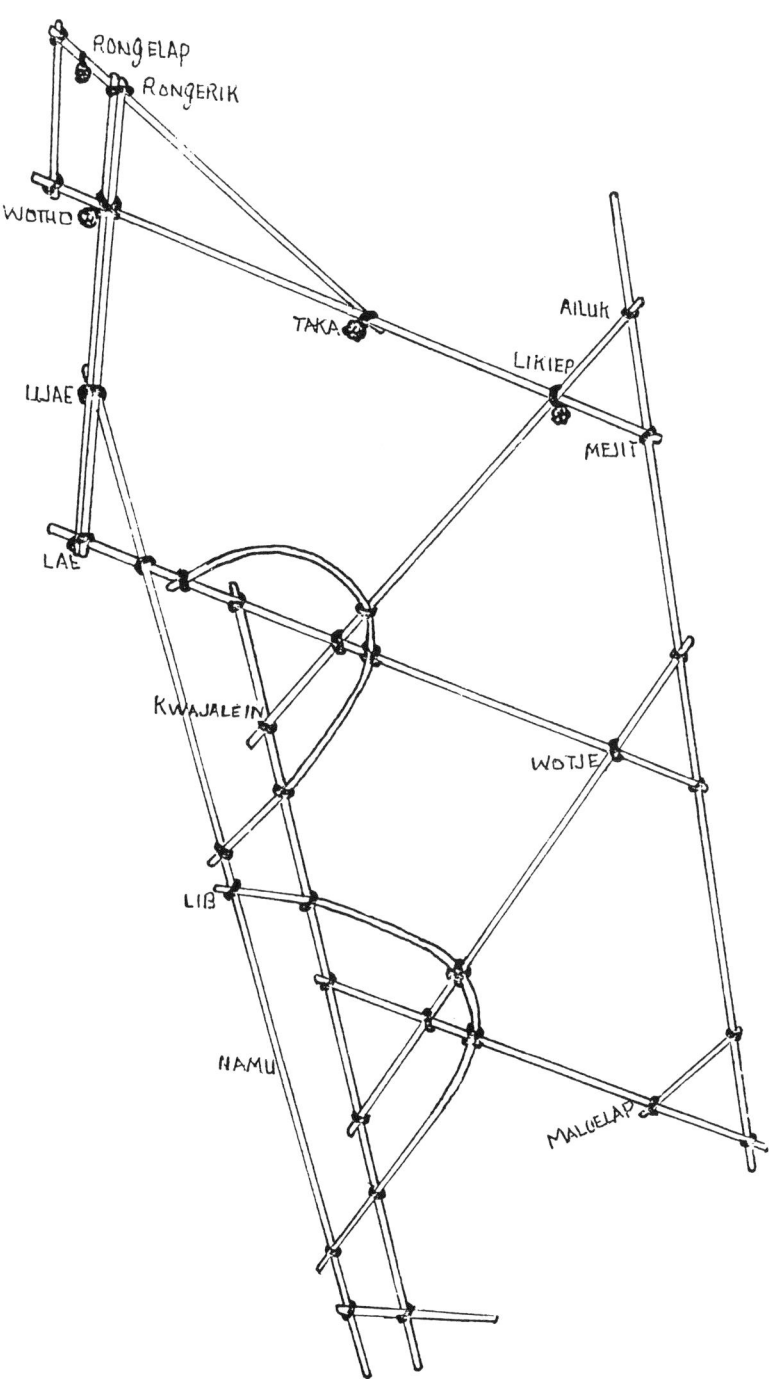

Marshall Nautical Chart

# *Related Readings*

Alpers, Antony, *Legends of the South Sea*, London, William Clowes and Sons, 1970.

Bernart, Luelen, *The Book of Luelen* (translated by John L. Fischer, Saul H. Riesenberg and Marjorie G. Whiting), Honolulu, the University Press of Hawaii, 1977.

Emory, Kennth P., "Myths and Tales from Kapingamarangi," *Journal of American Folklore*, Vol. 62, 1949.

Grey, Eve, *Legends of Micronesia*, Books I and II, Honolulu, Office of the High Commissioner, Trust Territory of the Pacific, 1951.

Hambruch, Paul, *Ergebnisse der Sudsee Expedition*, 1908-1910 (Pohnpei Southsea Expedition) Vol. I, Hamburg, Friederichsen de Gryter and Company, 1936.

Johnson, Margaret and Roy, *Life and Legends of Micronesia*, Murfreeburo, N.C., Johnson Publishing Company, 1980.

Kesolei, Katherine, *Palauan Legends*, Books I and II, Koror, Palau, Palau Community Action Agency, 1975.

Lawrence, Pensile and others, *Pohnpei Ni Mwehin Kawa*, (Old Pohnpei), Saipan, Trust Territory Printing Office, 1973.

Lessa, William A., *Tales from Ulithi Atoll, A Comparative Study in Oceanic Folklore*, Berkeley, University of California Press, 1961.

_____, *Folklore and Mythology Studies: 32, More Tales from Ulithi Atoll*, Berkeley, University of California Press, 1980.

Mangefel, John A., *Seven Legends of Yap*, Colonia, Yap, Education Department, n.d.

Van Peen, Marvis Warner, *Chamorro Legends on the Island of Guam*, Guam, Mariana Islands, Micronesian Area Research Center, 1974.

Uag, Raphael and Frank Malinksi, *A Legendary History of Yap*, Colonia, Yap, Education Department, Good News Press, 1968.

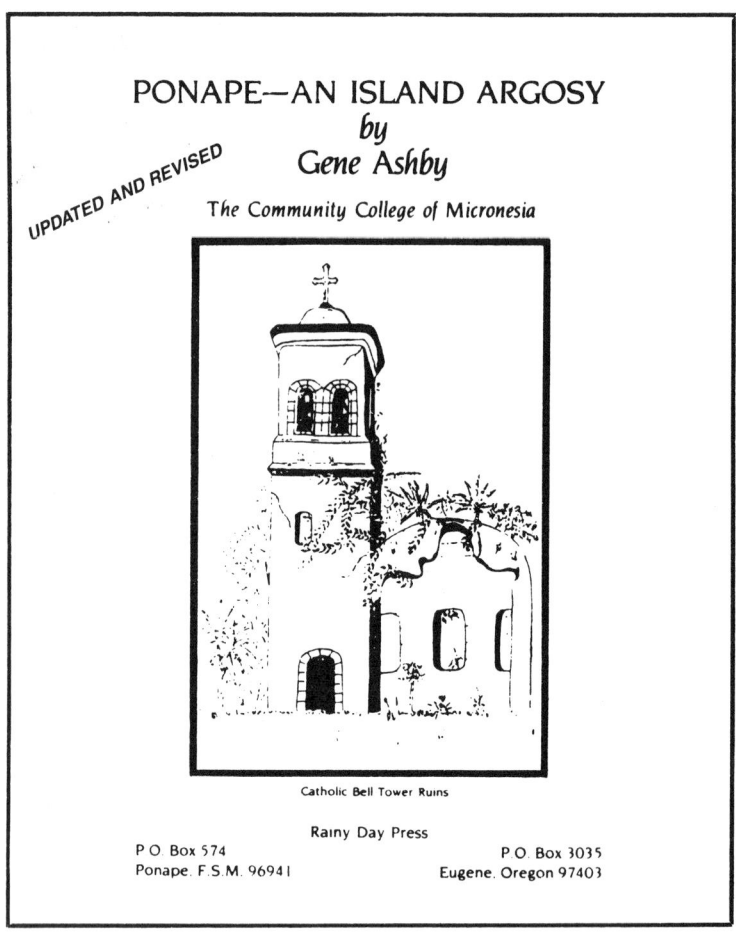

# PONAPE—AN ISLAND ARGOSY
### by
### Gene Ashby

*UPDATED AND REVISED*

The Community College of Micronesia

Catholic Bell Tower Ruins

Rainy Day Press

P.O. Box 574
Ponape, F.S.M. 96941

P.O. Box 3035
Eugene, Oregon 97403

History, natural features, flora and fauna, government and education, culture, customs and languages, places of interest, and a list of selected readings on the capital island of the Federated States of Micronesia in the Western Pacific Ocean.

Twenty-four maps and charts, and 30 illustrations.

*"**Ponape, An Island Argosy** tries to tell it all about the island, and very nearly does."*
—PACIFIC MAGAZINE

*"No library of Micronesia should be without it."*
—GLIMPSES OF MICRONESIA

**ISBN 0-931742-14-5**
**320 pages**
**$10.50**